The Art of Chinese Papercuts

TRADITIONAL CHINESE ARTS AND CULTURE

The Art of Chinese Papercuts

Zhang Daoyi

FOREIGN LANGUAGES PRESS   BEIJING

First edition 1989

Edited and Translated
By Ellen Hertz and Tang Bowen

ISBN 0-8351-1577-1
ISBN 7-119-00791-2

Copyright 1989 by Foreign Languages Press, Beijing, China

Published by Foreign Languages Press
24 Baiwanzhuang Road, Beijing, China

Distributed by China International Book Trading Corporation
(Guoji Shudian) P.O. Box 399, Beijing, China

Printed in the People's Republic of China

Contents

Foreword

The attraction of the traditional Chinese folk art of papercutting may lie in its apparent simplicity: a typical papercut requires no paints or brushes, only an ordinary pair of scissors or a knife, and a single sheet of paper. As the use of paper became well established throughout China, this art form came into being and has since enjoyed more than 1,500 years of popularity. Outstanding among Chinese folk arts, papercutting's influence in other fields and the number and variety of its products reveal the depth of its roots in popular culture as a means of beautifying the everyday environment of the broad masses of the Chinese people.

Papercuts can be seen everywhere in China. In many large cities one can find handicraft shops which sell papercuts characteristic of their area, usually rather delicate in design and made by local artisans from workshops or small factories. In smaller cities or market towns it is easy to find old women displaying every variety of papercut in their round bamboo baskets, cutting as they sell. These women specialize in making stencils for people to follow in embroidering shoes, children's hats and aprons. In the countryside, particularly in some of the northern provinces, colourful papercut "window flowers" cover the white paper which the peasants paste over the latticework on their windows. These "window flowers" tell traditional folk tales, depict popular characters from operas or plays, or portray mythical birds and beasts side by side with cuts of the well-loved domestic animals, flowers and plants from the peasant's immediate surroundings. These are the works of the peasants themselves, mainly at the hands of older peasant women or young girls, and seem to be windows into the hearts of the people, revealing to us their hopes and sense of beauty, and reflecting the sincerity of their feelings for life.

With its roots in the lives of the common people, the art of papercutting has a country charm which is both simple and honest. Currently in China, however, papercuts are not only a popular art form, but have also attracted the attention of professional artists, who use these themes of everyday life to enrich their own work. At the same time, these artists promote the development of folk papercuts, increasing the variety of themes, and broadening the range of applications for papercutting. We can see the effects of the use of papercuts not only in paintings, literary illustrations, comic books, book layout and design, stamps, slides, stage sets, frontispieces and endpieces for magazines, etc., but also in the art of movie making, where vivid papercut cartoons bring a new spirit of youth and vigour to the art of papercutting as a whole.

In recent years, as a number of papercut artists have gone abroad to exhibit their works, both the interest in and the market for Chinese papercuts have increased. This book is intended to provide a brief introduction to the origins and history, the style, the themes, and the techniques involved in papercutting, and is richly illustrated for your reading pleasure.

1. Origins and History

The earliest significance of papercutting lies in its combining a popular craft with ancient traditions and beliefs. According to ancient superstitions, offerings and ceremonies for the spirits were all carried out with green jade or silk which was buried after the ceremony. From the Wei (220-265) and Jin (265-420) dynasties on, paper was cut to symbolize money, which was then burnt during the burial ceremony. In 1959, in Asitana, in the Xinjiang Uygur Autonomous Region, silver-ingot-shaped pieces of paper money which had been scattered over the grave site were unearthed (Fig. 1). (Silver ingots served as a form of currency in ancient China.) Characters were found on the paper dating it to the eleventh year of the Zhanghe period (541). This embryonic form of papercutting cannot really be considered a true branch of the art, but it gives us a clue to its development.

Historical tales and legends provide us with other possible explanations for the origin of papercuts. The fifth emperor of the Western Han, Liu Che (156-87 B.C.), more commonly known as the famous Emperor Wu, was a highly superstitious thinker, and would spend huge amounts of money on religious ceremonies to show his respect for and ask the advice of the gods. It is said that at the death of his favourite concubine, Lady Li, he became so depressed that he could neither sleep nor eat, and spent every moment of the day pining after her. At that time there lived a man named Shao Weng, famous for his skill in divination and his knowledge of the occult. In an effort to console

Emperor Wu, he claimed he could summon back the spirit of Lady Li. Using paper, he cut out the image of the concubine. Then, at nightfall, he mounted the papercut behind a screen, illuminating it from behind with a candle to produce a figure so like Lady Li that Emperor Wu, looking through a second screen and unable to draw any nearer, felt even more sharply the agony of his loss. Perhaps, then, papercutting has its origins in these paper ghosts.

It seems reasonable to assume that the occasion of that first shadow figure should inspire the creation of papercuts. There is another story, however, which tells the tale of another Lady Li, a woman from Sichuan Province who lived during the Southern Tang period (937-975) of the Five Dynasties. As the story goes, she excelled in both literature and painting, and often sat until late at night before her window, deep in contemplation. One night

1. Paper money of the Southern and Northern Dynasties (420-589) cut in the shape of silver ingots.

she happened to notice the shadows of bamboo dancing in the wind outside, and, taking up her brush, she painted directly onto the paper covering the window. Seen by day, the paintings were lively and realistic. Many artists, inspired by this technique, began to use "shadow drawing" as a method of rendering bamboo, until it gradually became established as a legitimate branch of Chinese painting. If these "shadow drawings" were replaced by "shadow cutting", where an image in cut out of a piece of black paper, you have something like modern-day papercuts. In fact, the "shadow cuttings" so popular in Europe today could be considered just another form of the art of papercutting.

A third possibility for ancient uses of papercuts comes from a line of the poetry of Du Fu, the famous Tang Dynasty poet. In 755, Du Fu was forced to flee the rebellion in Chang'an, the capital city, and on the road was lucky enough to meet a local official by the name of Sun, who took him and his family in and cared for them. In the fall of 757, thinking back on this time, Du Fu wrote a poem entitled "Song of Pengya" in which he described the concern which his friend Sun showed him: "He warmed water for me to wash my feet; he cut paper and burned it to summon back my spirit." This poem records a kind of popular custom of the time. Believing that a traveller is bound to meet terrible things on his journey, people used papercuts to call back his spirit. It is imagined that this paper may have resembled long Buddhist streamers, and even today, using paper to make coloured flags or streamers is common in funerals.

As laws of historical development have shown us, there are no forms of artistic expression which simply spring into being from out of nowhere. Papercuts' roots in the superstitions and rituals of ancient times are not enough to explain the sudden occurrence of this craft, for every artistic form must have special characteristics which it shares with the other art forms which precede and inspire it. We will examine those influences in the following section.

Before Papercuts

Before the advent of papercutting, people had already learned to cut silver and gold foil, leather and silk, creating an art quite similar to that of papercutting. Precious silver and gold, pounded into leaf, have been excavated from sites as old as the Shang Dynasty (16th to 11th centuries B.C.) and used as ornaments. However, relatively few of these ornaments have been discovered, suggesting that at that time these metals were not as precious as jade. In 1955, near the city of Zhengzhou in Henan Province, a piece of gold leaf was unearthed decorated with the designs of a mythical *kui* phoenix, perhaps originally the ornamentation of some sort of vessel. This is the earliest material evidence that China was using gold for artistic purposes. And, because it too uses the method of cutting out spaces, it may be considered a distant ancestor of the papercut (Fig. 2).

In Guwei Village, Henan Province, was discovered a Warring States period (475-221

2. A mythical *kui* phoenix cut in gold leaf, Shang Dynasty (16th-11th centuries B.C.).

B.C.) piece of silver leaf of unusual beauty, cut in the shape of an arc (Fig. 3). It was patterned into a complicate swirl, possibly part of a circular decoration, with small holes along the border, but it is not clear what it was used for. We can see from these excavated objects that aside from the difference in materials used, the art and techniques of papercutting were virtually in existence already, and furthermore had already attained a high standard of excellence.

In the Han through Tang periods (206 B.C.-A.D. 907) this ingenious handicraft was used to decorate the expensive lacquerware of the time, and as backings for mirrors. This leafing involved cutting out designs in thin sheets of silver or gold foil, fixing them to the surface of the object to be decorated, applying several coats of lacquer and then polishing. The resulting gold or silver design was thereby smoothly inlayed in the layers of lacquer. On one such piece, there are traces of more than one hundred different designs in the shapes of people, animals, birds and clouds. (Fig. 4).

The craft of gold and silver leafing was further advanced during the Tang Dynasty, and the products even more brilliant. In Zhengzhou, Henan Province, a gold and silver-inlaid mirror with a diameter of 36.2 centimetres from the Tang Dynasty was

4. Copies of gold-foil designs for decorating lacquerware in the Han Dynasty (206 B.C.-A.D. 220).

unearthed. It has a knob on the back surrounded by cut-out silver leaf in the pattern of an eight-petaled lotus, which is in turn surrounded by winged people (spirits from fairy tales), flying phoenixes, flowers, birds, butterflies and cloud formations, all arranged in pairs (Fig. 5). This sort of ornamentation makes the most of the special characteristics of cut-outs, since gold can be used to delineate lines, and so, on a cut-out form, extra patterns can be traced. The intricacy of this work is compared to the fineness of a strand of hair and called "hair engraving".

3. Fan-shaped silver leaf of the Warring States period (475-221 B.C.) with openwork decorations (reproduction).

5. Gold and silver inlay on the back of a Tang Dynasty (618-907) mirror.

The art of leather cutting may also be related to papercuts. In ancient China, the highest rulers would wear deerskin hats ornamented with jade and pearls to show their position. In Liquan city, Shaanxi Province, a Tang Dynasty leather hat was unearthed which seems not to have been made for a king or emperor (Fig. 6). The hat is laced with cuts in the forms of intertwining branches, flowers and grasses, in complicated but still symmetrical designs. Though this involves a medium different from papercutting, the effect is equally satisfactory.

Ancient Customs

In the Tang through Song periods (618-1279) the popularity of cutting silk and gold, carried over from more ancient customs, developed into a kind of holiday ritual. People cut gold or silk into various patterns, including flowers, human figures and geometric designs, known as *sheng* streamers, to give and receive as gifts from one's friends and relatives on the first day of spring according to the lunar calendar. One of the only remaining flowered *sheng* streamers from the Tang Dynasty is still preserved in Japan's Seisouin Museum.

According to the Japanese *Records of Miscellaneous Possessions*, written in 856: "Found were two *sheng* streamers in the shape of humans, one with sixteen gold foil characters, the other with colours designed into a picture. The border is cut into a pattern.... The pieces are dated to the first year of the Tenpyo Houji period [757], the intercalary eighth month, twenty-fourth day" (Quoted from *Archaeological Notes on the Seisouin Museum*) (Fig. 7).

During the 1960s in Turpan County, Xinjiang, a piece of cut paper was unearthed from a collection of old tombs. It was cut into seven figures in line, called by archaeologists a "human *sheng*" (Fig. 8). From the looks of the paper cut it was done freehand and used as a burial offering, especially as it was found buried along with other paper money. Even though the craftsmanship is not superb, it still provides evidence of the age of this tradition, and establishes a directly link between the cutting of gold leaf and silk and the cutting of paper.

It seems plausible, therefore, that the art of papercutting developed out of pre-existing and related art forms. As the people who could afford expensive materials such as gold and silver to make ornaments like the gold ornament of the Jin Dynasty and the silver cutting decorating the kerchief of an unearthed figurine (Fig. 9), were limited to the aristocractic and literati classes, the common people were left to invent the art of cutting paper, a much cheaper material, themselves. As such, papercuts could be considered the popularization of gold leaf cuts, and represent a logical development out of this art form.

The Earliest Examples of Papercuts

From the perspective of an archaeologist, that ancient paper articles could be preserved at all, either passed down from hand to hand or

6. Copy of the design on a leather hat of the Tang Dynasty.

7. Tang Dynasty *sheng* streamer cut in
gold preserved in Japan's
Seisouin Museum.

8. Tang Dynasty "human *sheng*" cut in paper.

buried with tomb offerings, is extremely unlikely. In the last thirty years, Chinese archaeologists have discovered in the course of their excavations not only the earliest piece of paper but also a number of wholly preserved and basically complete papercuts. The discovery of these papercuts gives us models for researching the early stages of the art and extends the history of papercutting back about 1,500 years.

Turpan County, Xinjiang Uygur Autonomous Region is the site of the ancient city of Gaochang, an important point along the famous "Silk Road". In the nearby area of Asitana, a group of tombs has been discovered and archaeologists have already gone ahead with a number of excavations. Because of the arid climate of the Turpan Basin, the low precipitation level and the lowness of the water table, many paper and silk artifacts were preserved within these graves. In 1959 and after 1966, five specimens of papercuts were unearthed from three tombs of around the Southern and Northern Dynasties period (420-589). These five papercuts were as follows:

1. Pairs of horses cut into a circular design out of mustard-coloured paper. This was found in the same tomb as the above-mentioned silver-ingot-shaped paper money,

dating from sometime after A.D. 541 (Fig. 10 upper).

2. Pairs of monkeys cut into a circular design, also out of mustard paper. An inscribed memorial tablet unearthed at the same time dates this cut to the year A.D. 551 (Fig. 10 lower).

3. Octagonal design made of blue paper, unearthed from the same tomb as the horse cut (Fig. 11).

4. Circular cuts with a pattern of honeysuckle, 24.5 centimetres in **diameter**. Apparently once the colour of the jute paper it was made from, it has yellowed with age. A memorial tablet from the seventh year of the Yanchang period unearthed with it dates it to A.D. 567 (Fig. 12).

5. Circular cut in the shape of a chrysanthemum, 24.5 centimetres in **diameter**, cut from mustard-coloured paper. Unearthed at the same time as the above cut (Fig. 12).

All of these papercuts are cut by folding the paper before cutting, and exhibit a high level of technical proficiency. Though all these examples have been cut into symmetrical or circular designs, the artist has also paid careful attention to the interlocking of alternating patterns, which, from an artistic point of view, could not have been done without a lot of practice. In particular, the horse and monkey cuts have fitted the animals ingeniously into the circular layout. From a distance the cuts look merely like layered and elaborate patterns, but from up close we can see the leaps and bounds of living things.

These five cuts are probably the works of three different artists. They span more than twenty years, but all fold the paper before cutting. We can venture two possible responses to this: one is that the method of folding paper is best suited to making the most of the special characteristics of the paper, for the complicated patterns of presence and absence which result are not easily attained with non-foldable materials. The second

9. *Upper*: Gold ornament of the Jin Dynasty (265-420) decorated with two phoenixes holding a *sheng*. *Lower*: Silver cutting decorating the kerchief of a figurine of the Southern Tang Dynasty (937-975).

11. An octagonal design of the Southern and Northern Dynasties.

12. Circular cuts with the patterns of honeysuckle and chrysanthemum.

10. *Upper*: Pairs of horses cut into a circular design (reproduction). *Lower*: Pairs of monkeys cut into a circular design dating from A.D. 551.

7

popularization of paper to the period of these earliest examples there is anywhere from 200 to 400 years' history. During this long period, people must have been practicing and improving the art of papercutting. If we connect these discoveries with the stories of Emperor Wu's viewing the paper figure in the form of his concubine, and the brilliant works in gold leaf of the Han Dynasty, then we can be even more sure that this conjecture is reasonable.

Papercuts and Printed Textiles

Papercuts have had an influence on many other Chinese handicrafts, including one of China's most famous, the silk industry. China is the first country to have raised domestic silk worms and weave silk thread into cloth. As early as the late Shang Dynasty, more than 3,000 years ago, China was already making silk with lovely patterns. Later, with the appearance of silk brocade, silk products became even more sumptuous. However, the more lavish the brocade, the thicker the cloth and the more unsuitable it became for making clothing. To solve this problem, people began to paint patterns directly onto thinner silk. By the Western Han period, small pieces of wood were used to print designs, and from this came the process of dyeing patterns onto the silk.

There are many methods of dyeing, but the one that concerns us here is called "press dyeing". Press dyeing is a process which uses a wooden board with a cut-out pattern (stencil) pressing the cloth to be dyed in between two plaques and then, where there are holes in the plaques, coating the cloth with an agent to prevent dyeing, and, finally, immersing the cloth in dye. Later, paper stencils were used instead of wood. Some examples of these papercut prints have been discovered in Turpan, Xinjiang, and in Dunhuang, Gansu

comment connects with their unearthing: There were many funerary objects found along with these cuts, which, with a few exceptions, were all simulacra of everyday items, like for example, the small silk articles of clothing and pillows, some only centimetres large, as well as the paper-made shoes, hats and money. Therefore, we can infer that these round paper cuts cannot simply be ornamental, and are very possibly the simulacra of copper mirrors. If our inferences are not mistaken, these papercuts then reflect an ancient burial custom.

These five paper cuts are the earliest to be discovered in China to date, but that is not to say that before them there were no papercuts. These cuts are only representative of one area (Xinjiang), and one form papercuts can take (circular), and cannot tell us what the first papercuts looked like. The discovery of "Baqiao" paper which so stirred the archaeological world in 1957, in the suburbs of Xi'an in Shaanxi Province has decided that paper cannot be from later than the period of Emperor Wu of the Han Dynasty. With improvements in and popularization of the paper-making process by Cai Lun (?-121), paper began to be produced in great quantities in about A.D. 105. From the invention and

Province, and are mainly relics from the Southern and Northern Dynasties to the Tang Dynasty (420-907). The Tang Dynasty "printed gauze in the pattern of mandarin ducks under a tree", a white pattern on an ivory background, depicts a pair of mandarin ducks under a tree and is decorated with a background of small flowers in pairs, symbolizing the happiness and harmony of a perfect couple (Fig. 13). A second example is a silk pattern printed with hunting scenes. Limited, of course, by the printing process, the composition nevertheless uses a connected repeating pattern and preserves a sense of life and movement (Fig. 14). Other examples include silk decorated with a pattern of small flowers which are very similar to papercuts (Fig 15). We could call this process the younger brother of papercutting.

14. Hunting scenes printed on silk, Tang Dynasty.

13. A pair of mandarin ducks under a tree printed on gauze, Tang Dynasty.

15. Tang Dynasty silk decorated with a pattern of small flowers.

9

Happily, this brother grew to be a strong and healthy art of its own. After the Song Dynasty, the use of oil paper cut into designs and powdered starch made into starch paste to prevent dyeing were common. Examples of this type of cloth have been unearthed in Suzhou and Wuxi, Jiangsu Province, and in Shanxi Province (Fig. 16). With the great increase in the cultivation of cotton and the peasants making their own cloth, this type of printed material developed rapidly. Dyeing and printing, especially with the advent of indigo in the Ming period (1368-1644), became a national folk art, ranking with papercutting in popularity (Fig. 17 and 18). Even today, with mechanized factories producing great quantities of this printed materials, handwork has not been completely replaced, showing the depth of its root in popular culture. Many of the designs printed on this cloth still come directly from papercutting.

16. Copies of designs printed on cloth of the Song and Ming dynasties.

17. "Liu Hai Sporting a Toad," a design on
modern folk indigo print.

18. A peony design on modern folk indigo print.

Papercut Designs Fired onto Porcelain

Another of China's most famous handicrafts has been influenced by papercuts as well. Porcelain, the invention of the working people of ancient China, has used papercuts as a means of decorating the solid colour glazes.

By the Song Dynasty, the art of porcelain was quite advanced, with a great variety of colours and designs used, as we can see from the glazed patterned pieces coming out of Jizhou kiln at that time. Jizhou kiln was located in today's Jiangxi Province and in old records is referred to as the Yonghe kiln. Products of Jizhou kiln included not only red-brown and blue designs on a white background, but also the so-called "rabbit's hair" style of glazing in which silver white streaks as fine as rabbit's hair show through from under a glaze of dark reddish brown. Besides this interesting glazing process, Jizhou products are also remarkable for their use of papercut patterns. Jizhou porcelain take the form of vases, jars and, most characteristically, small teacup (Fig. 19).

20. Paper cuts of plum blossom, orchid and phoenix decorating Song porcelain of Jizhou kiln.

According to existing research, papercuts are used to make patterns on porcelain in the following way: the piece is first coated with a dark red-brown glaze, then the papercut is stuck directly onto this glaze and covered with a second layer of glaze, this time of a cream colour. Then the papercut is lifted off leaving the dark red-brown pattern. The cream glaze becomes a mass of what we have called "rabbit's hair" after firing.

It is really the use of designs from papercutting which gives folk porcelain its magnificence. Many different designs are used: an isolated branch of flowering plum or bamboo; a lotus or cluster of bamboo stalks; six-petalled flowers linked into a repeating pattern; animal figures — deer, mandarin ducks, butterflies, mythical birds like phoenixes, etc. (Fig. 20). These patterns are laid out in a variety of ways, in pairs, in the form of a tripod, in four-sided symmetrical patterns, or by simply covering the surface with a pattern or synthesizing the design into one overall effect. These pieces can also be decorated with Chinese characters organized into a good luck pattern, as, for example, "May riches fill your halls", arranged into the shape

19. "Rabbit's hair" porcelain bowl of Jizhou kiln, Song Dynasty.

of a loquat branch which had a symbolic meaning at that time (Fig. 21). However, for some unknown reason, porcelain using papercuts existed as an art for only a short time, and in the following hundreds of years there were no new advances in this field.

It was not until the Opium War of 1840-42 that at Humen Fort in Guangdong Province there was sited a pottery vat for holding gunpowder on which the words "Fort Gunpowder Barrel" were stenciled with papercuts. The characters had been cut with negative lines from a long strip of paper, and some of the strokes were not connected: after firing, the characters were dark, while the space under the paper showed the original colour of the white clay. During the last couple of years in Linyi and other places in Shandong, workers have resurrected the craft of using papercuts to decorate pottery, and cleared new paths for applying the art of papercutting.

The Appearance of Papercut Artisans

By the Song Dynasty, the Chinese feudal market economy was quite advanced and, in turn, promoted flourishing city life. During the Northern Song (960-1127) in the capital city of Bianliang (today's Kaifeng in Henan Province) and the Southern Song (1127-1179) in the city of Lin'an (today's Hangzhou in Zhejiang Province), business had reached an extremely advanced level, with every manner of shop, pedlar and restaurant crowding the busy streets. To meet the material and cultural needs of the citizens of different social classes, craftsmen in every trade gradually appeared, and in particular, skilled artisans. At that time papercutting was considered a form of "small business" that is an entrepreneur artisan with a small capital base. According to records in Zhou Mi's *Tales of the Old Capital*, there were more than 170 of these small businesses in Lin'an alone at this time, and among these a number of businesses were directly connected with papercutting, such as "character cutting, cut patterns, and shadow plays". According to this book, "each enterprise involves ten or more people, all dependent on their business for clothing and food. This type of enterprise cannot be found anywhere else".

Some of these papercuts were used for superstitious or religious rituals. During the Song Dynasty there were professional wizards who used papercuts in the shapes of dragons and tigers, called "dragon-tiger flags", to carry out various rituals meant to drive away evil. From the Yuan Dynasty on (1271-1368) in the area then called Wu (now the area around Suzhou in Jiangsu Province) during periods of

21. Good luck patterns with characters meaning "Long life, riches and honour" and "May riches fill your house," for decorating Song porcelain of Jizhou kiln.

13

prolonged cloudiness and rain there was a custom of cutting out of paper a young girl with a broom in her hand called "The Maiden Who Sweeps the Sky Clear" and then hanging her from the eaves of the house to pray for clear skies (Fig. 22). In the Qing Dynasty masterpiece *A Dream of Red Mansions* we can find many passages which help us to understand everyday life in ancient times describing cutting paper figures of people and ghosts for various rituals.

Ming and Qing dynasty notes and local records also chronicle some of the expert paper cutters of the time: "Zhao E of the Jiajing period (1522-1566) made gauze lanterns, from smooth paper which they cut into the shapes of flowers, bamboo and birds, cover with wax, and dye various colours. Gauze is used to sandwich the papercut, allowing light to shine through and making the papercut glow as if it is floating in a film of smoke, indistinguishable from real objects" (*Annals of Suzhou Prefecture*).

"Lin Wenyao, also known as Gangzhai, began to study as a child. He went blind at middle age and since has cut characters out of paper. His cuts are powerful yet fine. Rich housewives often buy his work to make into scrolls, trading fresh rice as payment. People have called these Lin cuts" (*Annals of Jiande County, Yanzhou Prefecture*).

Shi was Zhang Caigong's daughter. She was ingenious, and while talking to you could cut paper into fine spring flower, fall chrysanthemums, delicate grasses and weeping willows, almost magical in effect. Her papercuts for decorating boxes for women's toiletries are extraordinarily attractive, and to obtain one is considered gaining a great treasure (*Annals of Baoding Prefecture*).

The papercut artisans referred to in these passages — Zhao E, Lin Wenyao and Shi — are just the lucky few, among the thousands of papercut artisans, whose names were recorded. The names of the vast majority simply fell into oblivion. Because of the length of the history of papercutting, and the special characteristics of popular culture which make it self-propagating as well as self-extinguishing, the names of these artisans are by necessity few, and their works no longer to be seen.

22. "The Maiden Who Sweeps the Sky Clear."

The Many Uses of Paper Cuts

With the appearance of professional papercutting artisans, papercutting developed over the generations along two distinct paths. One path is that of the masses of the peasants who practise papercutting as a kind of amateur cultural activity in response to ancient traditions and rituals. The second path comes out of the first — that of professional artisans whose works have a purely aesthetic purpose, and who, over generations of innovation, have expanded the field of papercutting. Needless to say, these two paths are not unrelated: the former is the basis for the latter, and the latter is the sublimation of the former, making papercutting both a long-standing and well-established art. In the following pages we will examine some of the innovative uses of the new papercuts turned out by professional cutters.

In 1965 in Jiangsu Province, a Ming Dynasty folding fan was unearthed, made from a frame of bamboo strips with a double layer of cotton paper, on which was painted a layer of persimmon juice, giving the whole fan a brownish colour with gold flecks. If held up to the light, this seemingly simple fan reveals a beautiful papercut pressed between the two layers of paper. The papercut is mounted in the centre of the fan, and is a picture of "The magpie and the plum flowers announcing the arrival of spring" (Fig. 23). In the Song Dynasty (960-1279) book *Records of a Dream of Grandeur* by Wu Zimu, it is written that "various coloured shadow-flower fans" are for sale in the Hangzhou night market, undoubtedly the ancestors of the fan under discussion which dates to the period around 1506-1521.

During the Kangxi period (1662-1722) of the Qing Dynasty, there was a court painter named Zhu Yuandou who excelled in painting flowers in beautiful colours. One of his works, a New Year's scroll, is painted mainly with flowers in vases, firecrackers, lanterns and the forms of various ancient eating vessels and utensils. At the upper end of the scroll are hanging five multi-coloured papercuts, called "door hangings". "Door hangings" have evolved out of the spring streamers of earlier times. Song Dynasty's Chen Yuanjing in his

23. A Ming Dynasty folding fan decorated with a papercut.

Notes on Seasons of the Year describes as follows: "For the first day of the New Year, the people take black paper or black silk and cut it into forty-nine streamers, which form a larger streamer, and these streamers are either carried by the eldest member of the family or pasted to the lintel." Though the content of these traditions have changed from the original meaning, in form these customs are still followed today.

The Qing Dynasty began when the Manchus from the northeast of China entered the central plains and unified China under their rule. Following Manchu customs, papercuts became used as interior ornaments, and entered the court. The Kunning Hall in the Palace Museum in Beijing is the section of the court used by the Qing emperors for wedding chambers and the interior decoration was arranged according to Manchu customs. Black papercut "double happiness" characters were pasted on the corners of the wallpaper, the centre of the ceiling was decorated with black papercuts in the shapes of dragons and phoenixes, and the walls of the passages on either side of the main halls of the palace were decorated with flowered papercut at the corners (Fig. 24).

Also during the Qing Dynasty it became commonplace to use papercuts as a kind of stencil for folk embroidery. This included pillow cases, embroidered shoes, embroidered

25. "There will be a happy event ahead," a design for embroidery.

halters, children's hats and small bags. In, for example, the Hubei folk piece of papercut on a small bag, the outer edges are cut neatly and symmetrically. The design is of a magpie standing in a persimmon tree in fruit; in between the persimmon and the magpie is neatly fitted a stylized coin (Fig. 25). At that time this was a popular good-luck symbol. With the "magpie" (*xi que*) symbolizing "happiness" (homonym *xi*), the "persimmon" symbolizing "event" (both pronounced *shi*) and "money" representing "ahead" (both read *qian*), the message of the drawing is *xi shi zai qian* or "There will be a happy event ahead".

From the above discussion and other materials on the subject we can see that in the long history of Chinese arts and crafts, papercutting has gained inspiration from other art forms, and has, in turn, influenced other art forms. The reason it remains healthy and is developing after 1,500 years of history lies in its relation to both the customs of a given time period and to the crafts of artisans where it became a commonly used form of ornamentation. Considered historically,

24. Papercuts decorating wall corners of Kunning Hall in Beijing's Imperial Palace.

though recent popular folk papercuts are somewhat different in content, variety and use, papercutting still combines popular customs with artistic ornamentation, and in this way it is not only a continuation of a long tradition, but has a bright artistic future as well.

2. Patterns and Styles

The Ornamental Appeal of Papercuts

The folk craft of papercutting is one of many popular art forms. There are, of course, differences in skill and inventiveness, but overall, papercutting is relatively simple to master. That is not to say that it is easy to produce a work of value, for each product directly expresses the artist's perceptions and aesthetic sensibility. Walking through a northern village where each and every household shines with colourful window ornaments on the clean white paper covering the windows, one has the sense that this not merely a means of beautifying the peasants' living environment, it is a window into their lives.

Interestingly, China is not the only country to enjoy such a handicraft. Papercutting is a popular folk art among peoples of other countries as well. Popular in Europe, for example, are shadow puppets and silhouettes with their own specific artistic flavour, and shadow puppets used in movie-making are even more charming. Polish folk papercuts use mainly symmetrical imagery, and are considered by some to be the highlight of the various forms of European folk arts. Japanese folk cuts are devoted to traditional festivals and religious ceremonies, and also serve as stencils for printing and dyeing fabrics.

In any discussion of papercutting we cannot forget the great French artist Henri Matisse (1869-1954), who devoted the later years or his artistic career to the art of papercuts, creating innumerable brightly coloured works. Matisse believed that a pair of scissors could be more adroit than a pencil, that cutting directly out of coloured paper was like being a sculptor carving directly into stone. Because the material for papercutting was cheap and easy to obtain, Matisse called this craft "the one-cent toy", not at all disparagingly, for Matisse felt he had found the "supremely handy" method for painting in one connected movement. From this we can see that the value of a work of art is decided not by the price of the materials used or the intricacy of the workmanship, but by the feeling of life which a piece of work embodies.

Basic Characteristics

There are basically two types of papercuts, one using scissors, the other using a small knife. Because of the nature of papercuts, however, there two methods produce virtually indistinguishable cuts, and therefore can be talked about together. Papercutting is a formative art, which means it must put to best possible use the special characteristics of the necessary tools and materials. Because the image is to be cut out of and not drawn onto paper, the image must be designed in such a way that all the lines connect. There is a type of papercut in which the lines do not connect, but in these cuts all lines must be shortened so that the finished product holds together. Thus there are two possible ways to deal with the spaces in a papercut: the first is called "connected lines" and the second, "discreet lines". We see here what is unique to papercuts. The former kind of line has also been called "positive cutting", the latter, "negative cutting". Needless to say, a single papercut can use either of these methods or both simultaneously.

Papercuts are an extremely charming form of ornamentation. Unlike painting, which depicts objects in extreme detail, the beauty of papercuts lies in the exaggerated yet simple depiction on a flat surface of flowers, insects, animals and human figures. Just as Chinese painters pay great attention to the peculiarities of pen and ink, or Chinese woodcutters to the "feel of the wood", so papercuts have a certain "feel to the knife" or scissors, which is not to be found with other artistic media.

A Large Variety of Design

The design of a given papercut is intimately connected with its practical uses, which we can divide into four categories:

The first includes those papercuts meant for decorative effect which are pasted directly on windows, walls, lanterns and paper sculptures, such as window ornaments, wall ornaments, ceiling ornaments, smoke vents, lantern ornaments and door hangings.

The second includes those papercuts designed to line and decorate gifts, doweries and sacrificial offerings, such as happiness ornaments, gift ornaments, candlestick ornaments, incense burner ornaments and the Double Ninth flags for the festival on the ninth day of the ninth lunar month.

The third is used as stencils for em-broidering clothes, hats, shoes, pillow cases, bibs, sleeve embroidery and backbags.

And, the fourth is used as a stencil for indigo prints, which are used for clothing, quilt covers, door and window curtains, cloth wrappers, aprons and scarfs.

Of these four uses for papercuts, the first two are a direct use of the product and second two are used in conjunction with another art medium. Below we will introduce each product in more detail:

1. Window Ornament

For the most part, these papercuts are pasted onto the piece of paper covering a window, though now with the arrival of more glass windows to the countryside, these cuts can be pasted directly onto the glass. The windows of peasant houses in the north of China are designed with vertical and horizontal strips of wood, making various geometric designs; on top of this is pasted a layer of "skin paper" (the paper is treated with tong oil which gives it the illusion of transparency and makes it last longer). Every Spring Festival each family changes the paper on their windows, and covers the new white paper with colourful papercuts. The peasants have free reign in designing these window ornaments, for excepting the "corner ornaments" pasted to the corner of each window and the circular ornaments, there are no limits to the choice of theme or shape: animals, flowers or people, and sets of cuts telling the story of a play or a folk tale are all common (Colour Plates 1-4). Some window ornaments are adapted to the open spaces in the windows by dividing an entire cut into strips (Fig. 26) or quarters to be fitted to the form of the window (Fig. 27).

In the countryside in Shandong Province, many of the peasant houses have pomegranate trees growing in front of their windows. These peasants have invented a kind of papercut in

26. A window ornament.

the form of animals (gamecocks, pairs of horses or monkeys, etc.) which have the head or feet detached from the torso and not pasted flat onto the window but rather tied with a bit of string which serves as an axis; then the edges of the cut are linked with strings to the tree outside. When the branches move, the papercut moves likewise. There is another of these mobile papercuts, called a window flap which is pasted over the vent in a plate of windows (Fig. 28). Only the top edge is glued and the bottom portion is cut into a fringe which flutters in the breeze.

2. Wall Ornaments

In general, there are two kinds of wall ornaments. The first is pasted on the walls closest to the bed, or in the north of China where the peasants sleep on *kang* (plateform beds), pasted all around the *kang*. Sometimes they are pasted alongside folk woodblock New Year prints. A third type is pasted on the kitchen stove, and called "stove ornaments". These decorations are generally bigger than window ornaments, and come in both solid

27. *Kylin* unicorn, a window ornament.

28. Peony, a window ornament.

complete picture. Usually these screens are modelled after paintings or tell stories.

3. Ceiling Ornaments

The decorated ceilings of the north of China are made from pieces of sorghum stems used as a frame onto which is pasted paper. A newly constructed ceiling is clean and smooth, perfect for pasting large papercuts. These types of papercuts are usually made by folding the paper into symmetrical patterns. Usually a round, diamond or polygonal cut (Colour Plate 5) is placed in the middle of the room, and triangular cuts are used as "corner ornaments" at the four corners of the room. Some families paste long cut borders in red and black. Of course, red is used most commonly for weddings.

4. Smoke Vents

During the long, cold winters of northern China, peasant families close their windows as fast as possible, and light the fire. In order to avoid poisoning themselves with the fumes

colours and patterns. The flowers pasted around a *kang* usually tell a story with a plot so that one can "read" it as one is lying on the *kang*. Stove ornaments usually are good-luck characters such as "May the harvest be plentiful" or "May you have more than enough every year". The fishermen of the coastal towns of Fujian Province also cut the proverb "May the wind and the sea be with you" (Fig 29).

There is another kind of wall ornament, not commonly found, which is cut into the form of a screen, with the four pieces organized into a

29. "May the wind and the sea be with you"—a wall ornament.

21

from the coal they burn, a vent is cut out of one of the windows or the transom window. The mouth of the vent is always square or rectangular, and papercuts are made to fit their shapes and beautify the vent. These papercuts are called "smoke vents" and are usually adorned with geometrical patterns, or animals and plants (Fig. 30).

5. Lantern Ornaments

Before the widespread use of electric lights the traditional forms of household lighting were the candle lantern and the oil lantern. The cage of the lantern blocks the wind, and enables the lantern to be carried in the hand. There are two types of these lanterns: the first kind is square in shape covered with gauze, or shaped like a basket or like two tile pieces joined together commonly used in daily life and for weddings and other celebrations; the other kind is used for traditional holidays, and come in every size and variety — geometrically shaped or as flowers or animals. According to the traditional lunar calendar, the fifteenth of the first month is called the Lantern Festival. On that night, every family hangs its lanterns

out in front of its door, while larger lanterns are displayed in the square or public gathering place. Each child carries a small lantern in his or her hands and the holidays become a combination of an exhibition and a competition. Because the colours of papercuts are bright, and they allow light to pass between the cut out portions, they are the perfect form of decoration for these lanterns. Some are cut in the form of good luck characters, such as *fu* (fortune), or *xi* (happiness), or they are used to signal out the name of the owner, as for example "the Wang's" or "the Zhang's".

There are two outstanding forms of papercuts used to decorate these lanterns. The first is called "walking horse" lantern (Fig. 31) and the second is called "gauze lanterns". The "walking horse" lantern works on the principle of a gas turbine, and appeared as early as the Song Dynasty. The cut figures are attached to a sort of vane which is moved by the rising hot air currents caused by the flame. "Gauze" lanterns are made by placing a papercut in between two pieces of gauze which make up the covering for the lantern cage. These lanterns were especially popular in the southern part of China during the Ming Dynasty, and are often referred to in the records of this period. The cut flowers, bamboo, and birds floating in between layers of gauze look as if they are floating in smoke.

6. Paper Trinkets

There was a traditional artistic activity from old China of decorating burial objects with papercuts. It has virtually disappeared today. According to superstitions dating from the Neolithic period, after people died they went to another world but still needed various things from earth. Their relatives were held responsible for providing them with these daily wares, but by the Song Dynasty paper replicas of these household goods would be

30. "Smoke vents" adorned with lotus, fish and flowers.

31. Opera characters for decorating lanterns.

characters into them like "Best wishes for fortune and long life", "A model family", "Work hard for the Four Modernizations" or "Farm scientifically". These are either cut out of a single hanging, or made from four hangings put together, each with one character. Most hangings are red, although there is no limit to the possibilities for design and colour (Colour Plates 6 & 7).

The custom of hanging door hangings perhaps evolved out of the Tang Dynasty custom of cutting silk into "spring streamers". Throughout the country on Spring Festival, every household pastes red couplets with black characters of good luck on either side of their doors, and over the doors are pasted many-coloured hangings, which flutter, welcoming the new breeze and symbolize the arrival of spring.

made instead and then burned in the name of the deceased. Frames for furniture and utensils were made with bamboo, rushes, and stalks of sorghum and then covered with coloured paper and papercuts. The forms of papercuts quickly changed to adapt to these burial offerings and became called "paper trinkets".

7. Door Hangings

There are many kinds of door hangings. Shandong has a kind of door hanging that is made from connecting cuts, each cut like the cross-section of a carrot, called a "carrot hanging". In Jiangsu, many door hangings are made from red paper and are called "red hangings". This shape of hanging looks like a cut out silk flag, with a wide head, which is attached to the beams or over the door, and a row of tassels on the bottom. They usually follow neat geometric designs or good-luck patterns, and often incorporate good-luck

8. "Happiness" Ornaments

As we can see from its name, another kind of papercut is used for happy occasions, in particular, the marriage of a young couple. With the exception of the bride's vanity mirror, these cuts are not pasted on the objects they decorate. Instead they are simply placed on top of tea servings, soap dishes or hand basins to welcome the young couple into their new home. Most happiness ornaments are red, and there are strict rules for their shapes — round, square, diamond-shaped, peach-shaped or pomegranate-shaped. The inside of the cut is made up of various good-luck patterns and the effect is of a flower tucked within a flower (Colour Plate 11) (Fig. 32).

9. Offering Ornaments

In old China when people adhered to the traditions and ceremonies honouring the gods and ancestors, these papercuts were used to

32. Mandarin ducks among lotus—
a "happiness" ornament.

decorate ceremonial offerings. Some were even cut into the shape of serving trays, with animals and fruit to match pasted on the offering table (Fig. 33).

The most characteristic of these offering ornaments are what are called "pig's head" ornaments. The outline is in the shape of a pig's head, and inside various patterns of good luck are designed in the pig's eyes and nose (Colour Plate 8). Pig's heads are used to pay respect to the gods and one's ancestors, and are common in the coastal regions of Shandong and Fujian provinces. In the old society in Fujian Province, people made offerings to the God of Wealth to pray for good fortune. A common offering was chicken with a papercut of chickens back-to-back covering it (Colour Plate 10). Though this tradition has almost disappeared and papercuts are no longer used, from the original papercuts we can imagine the insecurity which the working people felt about their working and economic conditions and their desires for a secure and comfortable life.

10. Gift Ornaments

In the countryside, wherever an old person has a birthday, a new couple has a baby, or a friend or relative comes to visit, people always

bring gifts such as cake, "long-life" noodles, or eggs, and usually these gifts are decorated with some sort of papercut (Colour Plate 12). In the Chaozhou area of Guangzhou, these are called "cake ornaments" (Fig. 34). In the Fujian coastal regions, these papercuts are used as

33. An offering ornament.

34. A gift ornament.

1. Butterfly—a window corner ornament.

2. "Quadruple Happiness"—a window ornament.

3. Katydid and bottlegourd—a window ornament.

4. Bird and flowers—a window ornament.

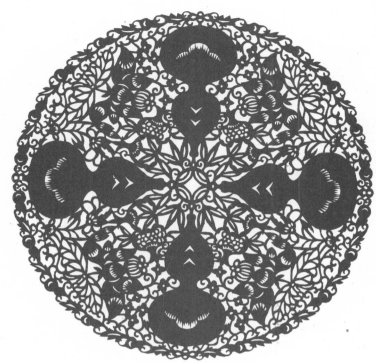

5. A round ceiling ornament.

6. A door hanging signifying
good fortune and wealth.

7. Door hanging with
plum blossom design.

8. An offering ornament in the shape of a pig's head.

9. A candlestick decoration.

10. Twin chickens.

11. Baby and lotus.

12. A gift ornament for cakes.

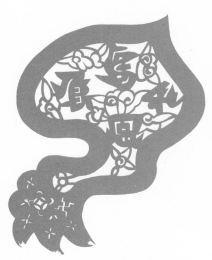

13. A ham-shaped gift ornament.

14. Tortoise.

15. A pillow decoration symbolizing
thriving domestic animals.

16. Tiger pattern for embroidery on a bib.

17. Decoration on a back sling.

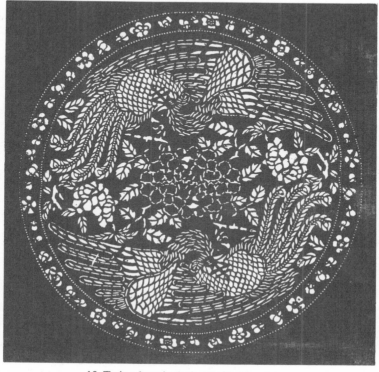

18. Twin-phoenix design for batik prints.

19. Twin-phoenix design.

20. Moneybag decoration.

21. A treasure bowl.

22. Flowers and bird.

23. Flying phoenix.

24. A chime stone.

25. Flower vase.

26. Flower vase.

27. The character *shou* (longevity).

28. Dragon, phoenix and flower designs for aprons.

30. Hat decorations.

29. Patterns for embroidery.

31. Swan, flowers and fruit—
decoration for a back sling.

32. "Liang and Zhu Change into Butterflies"—a wall ornament.

33. Twin swallows and magpies.

34. A large round papercut for decorating a handicraft article.

36. Zhou Yu (*left*) and Zhang Fei
in the Beijing Opera *Reed Marsh*.

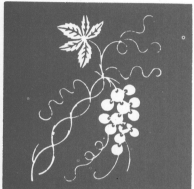

37. A scene from the opera *The
Story of the Western Chamber*.

35. Bamboo, chrysanthemum, orchid and grapes.

38. Flower vase—a window ornament.

39. Flower basket—a window ornament.

40. Floral pattern for a wood carving or lacquerware.

41. Cucumber.

42. Fish.

43. A hunter.

44. A screen of flowers and birds—a lantern decoration.

45. Snake encircling a rabbit.

46. Camel.

47. Ox.

48. Cat.

49. Rabbit.

50. Pig.

51. Hen and chicks.

52. Cowherd.

53. Fishing.

54. Eating candied fruit.

55. Playing a flute.

56. Pulling up a turnip.

57. The new bride returning home.

58. Lion dance.

59. Monkey with a peach.

60. Tiger.

61. Katydid and bottlegourd.

62. Katydid and turnip.

63. Quail.

64. Gold fish.

65. Mandarin ducks.

66. Double happiness.

67. God of Longevity.

68. Peach, bergamot and pomegranate.

69. Dragon and phoenix.

70. Carp jumps over dragon's gate.

71. Halberds, chime stone and fish.

72. "There will be immediate good luck."

73. Five bats surrounding a *shou* (longevity) character.

74. Cat playing with butterflies.

75. "The Two Immortals of Harmony."

76. "Mice Marry Off Their Daughter."

77. "Chang E Flies to the Moon."

78. Han Xiangzi, one of the Eight Immortals.

79. Monkey and Friar Sand, characters from *Journey to the West*.

80. Pig and Monk Xuanzang, characters from *Journey to the West*.

81. "Wu Song Fights the Tiger," an episode in the *Outlaws of the Marsh*.

82. "Daiyu Buries Flowers," an episode in *A Dream of Red Mansions*.

83. "The Whipping of Hong Niang," an episode in *The Story of the Western Chamber*.

84. "The Flooding of the Gold Mountain Temple,"
an episode in *The Story of the White Snake*.

85. Lan Caihe, one of the
Eight Immortals.

86. The Fairy Maid He,
one of the Eight Immortals.

87. "Zhaojun Journeys to the North."

88. "Su Wu Sent to Raise Sheep."

89. Dragon boat.

90. "Ridding the House of Vermins."

91. Pest-killing bottle-gourds—multi-coloured papercuts.

92. Peacock and flowers—a multi-coloured papercut.

93. Treasure bowl—a patchwork papercut.

94. Dragon flag—a patchwork papercut.

95. Peonies—patchwork papercuts.

96. Peace year after year
—door hangings.

97. Fish and baby on lotus pond—a patchwork papercut.

99. *Kylin* unicorn.

98. Phoenix with coloured background.

100. Pig with coloured background.

101. Painted opera mask—a hand-coloured window ornament.

102. An opera character—a hand-coloured window ornament.

103. A young woman—a hand-coloured window ornament.

104. Tiger—a hand-coloured window ornament.

105. Flower vase.

106. Katydid and cabbage—a
hand-coloured window ornament.

107. Lion.

108. Flowers.

109. Rooster.

110. Lion playing with balls.

111. Lion.

112. Twin birds.

113. *The Story of the Western Chamber*.

114. Magpies and plum blossoms with hand-painted details.

115. A flock of birds with hand-painted details.

116. "The Two Immortals of Harmony"
with woodblock-printed details.

117. Zhang Guolao, one of the Eight Immortals.

118. "The Goddess Scatters Flowers."

bands tying the thin vermicelli noodles around the middle (Colour Plate 13). In Shandong, to celebrate the birth of a boy eggs are pasted with papercuts or dyed red with white patterns. Furthermore, up until the 1950s the peasants in Fujian Province still preserved an ancient tradition which said that when giving gifts one should use the shapes of a tortoise to symbolize long life; tortoise-shaped cakes decorated with tortoise-shaped papercut (Colour Plate 14). This tradition, which has virtually disappeared in the main regions of China, had a 600-year history.

11. Candlestick Decorations

For weddings, birthdays and ceremonies to one's ancestors or to the gods it is popular to use candles stuck in tall candlesticks. Most of these candlesticks are made from tin and divided into many layers. On this candlestick, according to the significances of the occasion, various papercuts are attached, called candlestick decorations. For marriages usually a pair of phoenixes or mandarin ducks are used, or the character for double happiness (Colour

Plate 9). For birthdays usually the god of longevity or a sacred crane or the character *shou* (longevity) are used.

12. Incense Burner Decorations

In old society, ceremonies for the ancestors and the gods all involved incense burning expressing piety. Most incense is long and thin, and is called "thread incense", but there is another kind which is about as thick as chopsticks and covered with designs of seal-style characters, and called in the old days "seal incense". This kind of seal incense requires a stand, usually bell-shaped with slender bamboo points. The base of this incense burner is covered with colourful papercuts in the forms of people and fairies, as well as attractive designs and symbols (Colour Plate 117).

13. Double Ninth Flags

In folk traditions, the ninth day of the ninth lunar month, is a festival day. The weather is cool and crisp, and people all go out to walk in

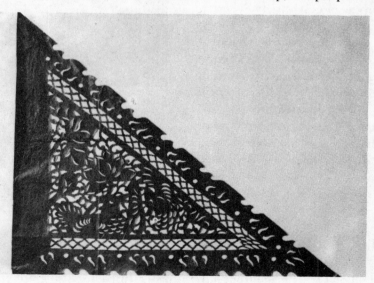

35. A Double Ninth Flag.

25

the autumn air and climb to the top of hills or mountains. To celebrate the festival there is a kind of triangular coloured streamer which children can play with or which is stuck in cakes. These "Double Ninth Flags" are often cut out or dyed with the patterns of dragons or tigers (Fig. 35). In the south on Moon Festival Day, on the fifteenth of the eighth lunar month, everyone burns incense for the moon, and in the incense burners are often stuck little flags of the same shape, also cut or printed.

14. Shoe Decorations

This type of papercut is used as a kind of stencil base for embroidering shoes. There are strict shapes for the outline, which can be divided into three categories: the first is a small circular pattern of flowers or small separate flowers embroidered onto the shoe's toe and called "tip flowers". The second, adapting itself to the shape of the shoe, is crescent shaped, and is called "toe flowers" (Fig. 36), and the third runs from the toe along the sides of the shoe and is called "saddle flowers" (Fig. 37). Of these, the second is most commonly seen and comes in the largest variety. There is also a kind of embroidery for the soles of shoes, used in the old society for funeral shoes, or embroidered onto the soles of socks. Though these sole flowers are not common any more, in the countryside to welcome the birth of a new baby peasants sometimes embroider the bottoms of the baby's shoes. The patterns of shoe decorations are usually clean and symmetrical, and sometimes are separated without leaving a space to serve as an indicator for embroiders to change the colour of the thread.

15. Pillow Decorations

Old-fashioned pillows were made from blue cotton, long and square at the two ends (hence

36. "Toe flower" to be embroidered onto a shoe's toe.

the alternative name "pillow end decoration"). Embroidered pillow cases are always made from red silk, and the multi-coloured embroidery is made into a square pattern. Next to the indigo-print pillow cover, it really has a folk appeal. The stencils for this embroidery are made from thin white paper called *lianshi* paper (used for calligraphy, and made from tender bamboo, giving the paper a pure white

26

37. "Saddle flower" for the
sides of a shoe.

colour and a fine texture). Most of them are cut
with knifes, though scissors will do as well, and
four pieces of paper are cut at once to make the
same pattern for the ends of two pillows. The
patterns fit into a square and can be arranged in
a variety of ways, but they are always
symmetrical and clean, harmonious and natural
(Colour Plate 15). Besides these square pillows,
there is also a kind of pattern for flat pillows for
children (Fig. 38)

38. Bergamot—pattern for
decorating a pillow.

39. Butterfly, peony and other flowers—pattern
for embroidery on children's hats.

16. Hat Decorations

The hats worn by children in the countryside
always display the young mother's wisdom and
skill. There are many styles — tiger heads, hats
in the shape of *ruyi*, an S-shaped ornamental
object made of jade, or lotus petals each
embroidered with its own kind of embroidery
in accordance with the shape of the hat. Some
are single patterns, some repeat patterns (Fig.
39).

17. Bib Embroidery

To prevent children from dirtying their
clothes with drool or food, mothers have
invented a kind of circular bib to be tied around
the infants neck. This also serves a decorative
purpose, and can be embroidered with
beautiful patterns. The outside of the bib is
divided into many sections, round, *ruyi*-shaped,
petal-shaped, or into many different shapes
which put together make a tiger (Colour Plate
16). Chinese people consider tiger "the king of
beasts", symbolizing fierceness and power, and
often use the character for tiger in their sons'
names. Mothers embroider this animal on their
little sons' bibs in the hopes that their sons will
one day have the spirit of a tiger.

18. Sleeve Decorations

The clothing of the women of minority
nationalities from the southwest of China, such
as the Miao nationality, the Dong nationality,
the Yao nationality, are extremely beautiful,
often embroidered or dyed in ways peculiar to
these nationalities. Some of this embroidery
uses papercut patterns as its basis. This
embroidery is used principally to decorate the
cuffs of sleeves, and is almost always flat and
full of intricate patterning in the shapes of
dragons and phoenixes, sparrows, butterflies,

etc. They are usually either symmetrical or balanced in some way, with a great variety in styles (Fig. 40). Though these are called sleeve decorations, they can also be found on trouser bottoms.

19. Back Sling Decorations

This is a kind of decoration used to decorate back slings with which minority women carry their babies on their backs. The sling is usually square, sewn up at the four corners with bands. The embroidery on the sling is all made from papercut models, patterned with a circle inside a square, and sometimes cut into round or polygonal flower wreaths (Colour Plate 17). From the decorations on back slings we can get a glimpse into the heart of the mother who embroidered it. The lifelike animals and birds made from strand after strand of thread are all signs of the mother's love for her child, and her hopes for his or her future happiness.

20. Indigo Prints

This is a technique using indigo dye to make designs on fabric. Cut the oiled paper into a pattern and then with a mixture of lime, starch and water make a dye-preventing agent, cover the material and immerse it in the dye, and then dry it in the air. When it is dry the dye-preventative can be scraped off to reveal white

41. Grass—a pattern for indigo prints.

patterns on a blue background (Colour Plate 18). Most of the paper stencils for dyeing use negative lines. If one makes two stencils, the first the opposite of the second, one could produce blue flowers on a white background (Fig. 41). Since these techniques of folk dyeing principally involve batiking, most people do not consider this a sideline of papercuts. In fact, like embroidery, it is one use of papercuts, and though the end product is a piece of material, the effect is similar.

A Distinctive Style

The style of Chinese folk papercutting is directly connected to its unique artistic vocabulary. The naivete of the forms, the force of the designs, the brightness of the colours and the restrictions on the tools and material used all reflect the working people's ingenuity and desire for beautiful surroundings.

The 6,300-kilometre Yangtze River divides China into north and south. Northern papercuts are characteristically "simple and vigorous" while southern papercuts are

40. Phoenix and peony—
a sleeve decoration.

"ingenious and refined". Popular papercutting can be classified into two schools according to these stylistic differences. At first glance, these papercuts are simply a means for the peasants to beautify their environment, but on closer examination we find that differences in lifestyles are captured by the different styles of the works. Large or minute, coarse or delicate, exaggerated or realistic, plain or gaudy, each expresses something different from out of the lives of the creators.

1. Size

Interestingly, papercuts vary in size from those big enough to decorate an entire door to those as small as a finger. The "Lion Pavilion" cut by the famous papercutter Rui Jinfu from Jiangsu Province is about one metre high, and extremely complicated and vivid. It depicts a famous moment in the classic *Outlaws of the Marsh*, when the hero, Wu Song, revenging his elder brother, throws the despot Ximen Qing out of a second-storey restaurant window. It has borrowed the characteristics of the Ming-Qing dynasty woodcut illustrations, as well as preserving the traditional style of painted scrolls (Fig. 42). A contrasting example is the set of works by a peasant woman from Shandong Province who has cut tigers, sheep, rabbits, chicken, magpies, quail, monkeys, etc., each no more than 2-4 centimetres high (Fig. 43).

2. Coarse vs. Refined

Coarse and refined represent two distinct schools of folk papercuts. Coarse papercuts are sparsely cut, bold in their simplicity, and give a sense of the strength of the subject matter (Fig. 44). Refined cuts look like weaving, lavish and intricate, but never overdone (Fig. 45).

3. Exaggeration vs. Realism

Exaggerated forms have ornamental value, while the appeal of realistic cuts lies in their being true to life. Take, for example, two papercuts of a cock: the first is from Shandong Province (Fig. 46). Though the lines are very regular, they seem quite realistic. The cock stands looking straight ahead, one claw raised, giving one the impression of strength and vitality. The second is from Shanxi Province (Fig. 47), and uses exaggeration, particularly in delineating the muscles of the cock's thighs. The most interesting part, however, is a rabbit, cut into the cock's mid-section, which acts as a foil for the strength of the cock. This almost romantic portrayal, by not adhering to a realistic depiction of the object, expresses

42. "Lion Pavilion"—a papercut depicting an episode in the novel *Outlaws of the Marsh*.

43. Window ornaments of small animals.

through exaggeration the spiritual world of the artist.

4. Plainness vs. Gaudiness

Most folk papercuts have a tendency to use rather simple methods and designs: the forms are cut in solid colours, mainly bright red. However, papercuts designed for specific uses which aim for pomp are sometimes made entirely of aluminum foil, decorated with many colours, as with the paper trinkets from Foshan, Guangdong Province (Colour Plates 98, 99), or the incense burner decorations in Nanjing.

China is a vast country. The papercuts produced in different regions bear different characteristics. These regional characteristics are very well illustrated in the following examples from Shaanxi (Fig. 48, 49), Gansu (Fig. 50), Shanxi (Fig. 51), Henan (Colour Plates 107, 108), Hebei (Colour Plates 105), Shandong (Fig. 52) (Colour Plates 23, 96), Heilongjiang (Fig. 53), Jilin (Fig. 54), Hubei (Colour Plate 20), Anhui (Colour Plate 19), Jiangsu (Colour Plate 22), Zhejiang (Colour Plate 25) (Fig. 55), Fujian (Colour Plates 21, 24) (Fig. 56), Guangdong (Colour Plate 26), Hunan (Fig. 57), Sichuan (Fig. 58), Yunnan (Colour Plate 27), Guizhou (Colour Plates 28,

44. Cabbage and katydid—
a window ornament.

46. Cock—a window ornament.

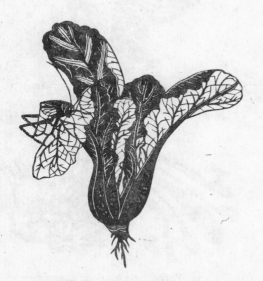

45. Katydid and cabbage—
a window ornament.

47. Cock—a window ornament.

48. Opera characters—window ornaments from Shaanxi Province.

50. Eagle—a window ornament from Gansu Province.

51. Opera characters—window ornaments from Shanxi Province.

49. Butterflies—a "smoke vent" ornament from Shaanxi.

53. Phoenix—a window ornament from Heilongjiang Province.

52. Lily—a window ornament from Jiaoxian, Shandong Province.

54. A door hanging from Jilin Province expressing hope for a good harvest.

55. Window ornaments from Zhejiang Province depicting scenes from operas.

56. "Happiness" ornaments from Fujian Province cut in the shapes of a fish and two pomegranates.

57. Embroidery patterns for shoes from Hunan Province.

58. Shoe decoration from Sichuan Province.

30), and Guangxi (Colour Plates 29, 30).

In addition to regional differences in style, papercutting has been heavily influenced by China's many minority nationalities. In the north, the Manchus had an influence, especially during the Qing Dynasty when palace customs could set national tastes. In the south, the Dai, Miao, Tong and Naxi minorities are especially famous for the use of papercuts as stencils for embroidery, and have their strongest influence in this field.

Famous Papercut Artists

The majority of papercut artists are, of course, peasant women, who cut paper as a hobby. However, in certain areas and cities there are also workshops of a limited scale whose artisans cut paper either as a sideline activity or as a full-time profession. Some of these professional artisans are quite outstanding, and their skill and sense of design represent the culmination of the art. Below we shall introduce a few famous professional artists, and peasant hobbyist.

Wang Laoshang (1890-1951)

Born in Yuxian, Hebei Province, he worked with a knife and is most famous for his use of spot dyeing. His cuts usually tell the story of a play or opera, and their development has been heavily influenced by water colour woodblock prints from Hebei's Wuqiang County. Wang Laoshang was an ordinary peasant and studied papercuts from his childhood. By the age of twenty he was already a good artisan, and after another forty years of hard work he became the most famous artist in his area. He illustrated over two hundred operas and plays in his lifetime, and cut more than six hundred different characters, as well as a large collection of flowers and bird window ornaments (Colour Plate 36) (Fig. 59). His works are lively, realistic and well executed, and the colours bright but harmonious. Furthermore, he made use of the techniques of woodblock prints which allow for differences in intensity and shade of colour creating highlight and contrast.

Zhang Yongshou (1905-)

From Yangzhou, Jiangsu Province, he is the fourth generation of professional papercutters

59. A portrait of Wang Laoshang.

60. Zhang Yongshou.

in his family. He started cutting when he was twelve, specializing in stencils for embroidery.

Zhang Yongshou has summed up the main skills of papercutting in these five words: circle, point, square, space and line. "The round parts should be as round as the harvest moon, the points as sharp as an awn of wheat, the square parts as square as a brick, the spaces as clean as a saw's tooth, and the lines like whiskers. In 1958, he illustrated the anthology of poems *Let a Hundred Flowers Blossom* compiled by the great modern poet, Guo Moruo, with 101 different cuts of flowers and grasses. Recently he has finished a collection of one hundred chrysanthemums and a collection of butterflies and flowers. In his sixty-year career Zhang Yongshou has cut more than ten thousand papercuts, concentrating on chrysanthemums. In 1979 the Chinese Ministry of Light Industry honoured Zhang with the title of "Master Handicraft Artist" (Colour Plate 35) (Fig. 60).

Zhang Jigen (1921-1983)

From Jintan, Jiangsu Province, Zhang Jigen spent much of his time as a papercutter in Nanjing, and was a Master Craftsman at the Nanjing Folk Crafts Workshop. His wedding papercuts are solid but the rigid outline hides many free and imaginative forms, often with traditional symbolic meanings carefully inserted in the cut by a method called "cutting within a cut" (Colour Plate 33).

Rui Jinfu (Dates of birth and death unknown)

Rui Jinfu was from Yixing, Jiangsu Province. Born into the peasantry, his parents sent him at the age of fourteen to a professional artisan, Mo Chunbao, as an apprentice in his workshop. After seven and a half years of hard work, he learned the art of papercutting, sculpting and decorative design. His papercuts are used mainly for decorating lanterns, but his later works were used for screens as well. His larger works are based on the plots of the Chinese classics, like *Outlaws of the Marsh* and *Tales of the Three Kingdoms*. The layout is complicated and interwoven, and he knows how to use the characteristics of painting without losing the feel of the paper. He is particularly good at using *jintang* (lines which connect the border to a central figure or scene) and *huakuang* (decoration around the edge of the work) to set off the theme and story (Colour Plate 32).

Jiang Genhe (1873-)

From Chaozhou, Guangdong Province, he devoted his entire life to the art of papercuts, and in 1957 at eighty-four he was still working. The opera characters he cuts are exaggerated and their postures full of rhythm. His specialities are partial folding and separated cutting methods, which enrich the variety in the design. His two most famous works are "Liang Shanbo and Zhu Yingtai" and "The Story of the Western Chamber" (Colour Plate 37).

Li Yaobao (1892-1983)

Famous papercutter from Quanzhou, Fujian Province. His works are robust and the lines fluent. The content of his cuts all come from traditional folk patterns, such as flowers, birds and human figures from antiquity. Most of his cuts were used in constructing houses and furniture as stencils for lacquerware or carvings. His works are not limited in their appeal to the southern Fujian Province but are exported to Southeast Asia (Colour Plates 34, 40, 44).

Gao Yousan (1893-1981)

Born in Jiaoxian, Shandong Province, he was a famous papercutter of the locality. His single-coloured cuts are vigorous and forceful, and his multi-coloured ones known for their exquisite cutting and colouring. His works used to be exported to Europe together with laces produced in the Jiaodong area of Shandong Province.

Cong Lin (1918-)

From Penglai, Shandong Province, Cong Lin was born in a village near the county seat. Her elder sister and sister-in-law both cut well, and from them she learned to love the art. At thirteen she was already quite an expert artisan. Both in her choice of themes and in her sense of design, she has excellent artistic instincts. In 1954, the Beijing Zhaohua Art Publishing House printed *Cong Lin's Collected Window Cuts* (Colour Plates 38, 39).

Chen Yuan

From Pujiang, Zhejiang Province, she was a

peasant woman who cut paper in her spare time. She used a huge variety of motifs, including flowers, fruit, fish, birds, and human figures from stories. In 1960 the Light Industry Press printed some of her works in *Collection of Papercuts from Pujiang* (Colour Plate 41).

Yan Xifang (1898-1979)

From Anzhai, Shaanxi Province, originally this woman had no name of her own, so people had to call her by her daughter-in-law's name. Her work is not heavily cut, though the workmanship is exquisite. Even in her 80s, she still insisted on covering all the windows and decorating the *kang* base with papercuts. Just before dying she gave a great bundle of papercut designs to her daughter-in-law, saying: "I am afraid I didn't leave anything for you. All my life I have loved papercuts. I leave these papercuts to you, but I have no other possession." (Colour Plate 45).

Wang Zhanlan (1908-)

Also from Anzhai, Shaanxi Province, she cuts paper in a primitive style which captures a spirit of boldness in a few, quick strokes (Colour Plate 43).

Hu Fenglian (1923-)

Hu Fenglian is another papercutter from Anzhai, Shaanxi Province. She can paint, embroider and cut paper, and it was said that "when she gets on the *kang*, she picks up her scissors; when she gets down, she picks up a sickle." Her style is clean and flowing, and she is best at birds, flowers and animals (Colour Plate 42).

3. Themes and Content

From the themes of peasant papercuts we have a glimpse into the themes of peasant life. Oddly, in the huge variety of works that represent folk papercutting, one finds that the peasants rarely depict themselves or scenes from the fields or work place.

Many of the cuts, instead, are of human figures from plays, operas or traditional stories, as we see in many of the following plates. Aside from these two themes, most papercuts are of domestic animals (Colour Plates 46-51) (Fig. 61-63). The only exceptions are those papercuts that throw sidelights on the life of the peasants, such as herding cattle, feeding pigs, horseback riding, picking lotus, fishing, chopping wood, playing the flute, or scenes of the new bride returning home on the family wagon (Colour Plates 52-57) (Fig. 64). Peasant women often cut pictures of eagles catching rabbits, monkeys stealing peaches, crickets eating cabbage, or insects and gourds. They often distort the proportions of the objects they depict, exaggerating the forms of their subject matter to make the cuts more lively and suggestive (Colour Plates 59, 61) (Fig. 65-67).

The peasants' desire for a prosperous and stable life is recorded in many forms of folk culture, ancient and new. The relatively recent mechanization of the countryside and the increased availability of consumer goods have not changed the traditional themes of papercuts. Today, after a day of labour in the fields, the peasants gather in the living room to watch television or listen to the radio. But most of their papercuts are still based on traditional themes such as "A Good Harvest of the Five Grains", "May You Have More Than Enough Every Year" and "Prosperity for People and Animals". They use phenomena from their surroundings to express these themes and wish for improvements in the future.

Flowers, fruit and living creatures are also among the subjects that appear in papercuts, such as peony, lotus flower, chrysanthemum, plum blossom, orchid and narcissus (Fig. 68-70); peach, persimmon, pomegranate and turnip (Fig. 71); magpie, pigeon, quail, mandarin ducks, peacock, crane, lion, tiger, spotted deer, monkey, golden fish, carp and butterfly (Colour Plates 58, 60, 62-65) (Fig. 72).

Good-luck Characters and Sayings

"May fortune be with you" blesses people with good fortune, goodness, joy, and fulfilment of their every wish. People use these themes either to cut paper directly into characters or to express their meaning through the use of symbols and punning on historical stories, related animals, plants and objects. The following are some of the most common expressions of good wishes and their symbols.

Fu (Fortune)

Fu means good fortune and can be expressed either through a direct rendition of the

61. Ducks.

64. Herding goats—a window ornament.

62. Goat—a window ornament.

65. Mice pulling a cart—a window ornament.

63. Horse—a window ornament.

66. Monkey and goat—a window ornament.

67. Cabbage and katydid—a window ornament.

69. Basket of flowers.

68. Lotus flowers.

70. Hydrangea.

40

71. Pomegranate—a window ornament.

73. Papercuts of the character
fu (good fortune).

72. Lion—a window ornament.

character itself (Fig. 73) or through puns on objects with homophonous characters, such as bats (bian*fu*), or bergamot, a kind of citrus fruit used in Chinese medicine and called "*foshou*" in Chinese. It is interesting to note that through this process, an animal such as the bat can have very different connotations, depending on the culture it is being considered by: in the West, bats are considered to be an omen of evil, a "night spirit", and Aesope characterizes the bat as two-faced; but in traditional Chinese symbolism, because of the pun on the homonyms *fu* and because of hearsay spread by priests who believed the bat was able to make people live longer, ever since the Ming-Qing period it has been an important decorative motif (Fig. 74). Bergamot, which got its Chinese name "Buddha's hand" because it looks like an old man's fingers, has attracted people through its golden-orange colour and its fragrance (Fig. 75). Furthermore, since it is similar in sound to the character for fortune, it has come to represent that meaning in papercuts. Add to this the pun on the second character of its name (*shou*, hand, and *shou*, long life) and this fruit represents the double goodnesses of fortune and long life.

74. Bat—a window ornament.

75. Bergamots—a window ornament.

Lu (Prosperity)

The original meaning of this character was an official's salary, and slowly it has evolved to mean prosperity generally. In the symbolism of papercuts, artists have borrowed the sound *lu* (meaning white-spotted deer) (Fig. 76). In olden times people claimed that deer could seek out magical herbs, and were the mounts of the gods, often depicted with a branch of ganoderma in their mouth supposed to have the power to promote long life. For this reason, deer have come to be associated with Chinese medicine, and are often called "magic deer".

76. Deer—a window ornament.

Shou (Longevity)

This character has many hundreds of forms — in regular script, in cursive script, and in one of its many archaic forms, and so is a kind of design in and of itself (Fig. 77). It can also be represented by the God of Longevity or the peach of immortality. The God of Longevity is depicted as an old man with a protruding forehead and huge ears (Colour Plate 67). According to ancient mythology, anyone who eats the peach of immortality is able to live a long life (Fig. 78).

Xi (Happiness)

Happiness has a general meaning of joy or good fortune, and a specific meaning of marriage and the birth of sons. For marriage, two *xi* characters are connected into a "double happiness" (Colour Plate 66). The images which can stand for *xi* are principally the magpie (*xi*que) and the spider (*xi*zhu). The magpie is a common bird in China, often seen resting on the branches of trees in people's courtyards. From the Tang Dynasty on, people have considered the call of a magpie a good omen. The *xizhu* is a kind of tiny spider. In old China people believed that if this insect fell on your clothes a good friend would come soon to visit (Fig. 79).

78. Peaches—a window ornament.

77. The character *shou* (longevity) in an archaic form for decorating a burial object.

79. "Heaven-Sent Happiness."

43

Ruyi

This originally was a kind of instrument for scratching, made from bamboo or wood with a head in the shape of a hand. Later the ends of the heads were made in the shape of a ganoderma or other precious plants, and its handle was curved, often embedded with jade, ivory, gold or silver. The *ruyi* acted as a kind of toy which the ancient emperors gave to their officials. For this reason it has come to symbolize power. Decorative designs and papercuts often use this or some variant to mean "Things will go according to your wishes", a pun in Chinese (Fig. 80).

Panchang

This design got its inspiration from knitting or weaving, and involves curved but symmetrical lines braided into six knots with the head and tail of the design meeting to form a circle. It symbolizes ever-changing continuity (Fig. 81).

Fangsheng

Originally, a kind of head decoration or ornament worn by women in the olden days, the basic shape of this trinket is two interlocking diamonds. It symbolizes excellence and unity of purpose (Fig. 82).

Love

In traditional ornamentation, symbols for love are many and varied. Among papercuts, mandarin ducks, the dragon and the phoenix, and butterflies and flowers are commonly seen. Mandarin ducks are aquatic birds which go everywhere in pairs. In ancient China these were called "matching birds", and became a natural symbol for love and the harmonious relations between husband and wife (Fig. 83). Butterflies flying among flowers give people a

80. *Ruyi*, a symbol meaning that "things will go according to your wishes."

81. *Panchang*, a symbol meaning "ever-changing continuity."

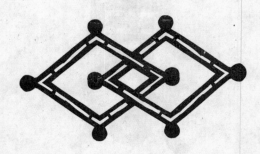

82. *Fangsheng*, a symbol of unity of purpose.

44

83. Mandarin ducks.

feeling of beauty which makes this scene a natural symbol for love. The dragon and the phoenix are both mythical beasts with magical powers; the dragon has scales and a beard and possesses the power to stir up the clouds and make rain. The phoenix has the head of a chicken, the neck of a snake, the chin of a swallow, the back of a turtle, and the tail of a fish, and is brightly coloured. In feudal society, the dragon and the phoenix symbolized the emperor and empress, but also implied love. In congratulating people on their marriage, one can say, "The dragon and the phoenix signify good fortune" (Colour Plate 69).

Jixiang (Auspiciousness)

In ancient Chinese, xiang and yang (sheep) were the same sound, and the later was invested with the meaning of the former. From the Han Dynasty (206 B.C.-A.D. 220) painting sheep to represent good fortune became a custom. The character ji also has a homonym in ji (chicken) which is sometimes used to the same effect as sheep (Fig. 84).

Jiqing (A Happy Occasion)

This pun uses two kinds of instruments, a ji and a qing to symbolize celebration. The ji (halberd) is an ancient weapon with a

spearhead and a crescent-shaped blade on a long handle. The qing (chime stone) is a kind of ancient musical instrument made from stone or jade, and later from metal (Fig. 85). If a fish (carp) is added, it also symbolizes good fortune (Colour Plate 71).

Shuangquan (Double Good Luck)

This symbolism is based on two pieces of copper coins interlocked to read shuang (pair) qian (money) (Fig. 86), which is close to the sounds for the words shuangquan meaning, literally, double completeness. Sometimes the coins are replaced with bats and peaches or the character for "good fortune" or "longevity" (Fig. 87).

Wufuqingshou (The five good fortunes celebrate your long life.)

Usually five bats surrounding a shou character or a peach of longevity (Colour Plate 73). The five fortunes are referred to in a collection of documents from ancient Chinese history as: longevity, prosperity, health, good morality, and death by old age. This was what the ruling class of the period wished for in their life, and of course this kind of thinking influenced the common people as well. In the people's New Year's paintings the five

84. Rooster.

85. *Jiqing*, a symbol of good fortune,
for decorating a pillow.

fortunes are: *fu* (fortune), *lu* (prosperity), *shou* (longevity), *cai* (wealth) and *xi* (happiness), but this is a rather common explanation, which goes beyond the basic meaning of the classics.

Maodiechangshou (Long Life)

There is an old Chinese vocabulary used specifically for old age as follows: "At seventy you are called *mao*, at eighty you are called *die* and at one hundred you are called *qiyi*." Two animals with homophonous names are the cat and the butterfly, and therefore pictures of cats playing with butterflies are not only interesting in their own right, they also carry the implied meaning of wishing someone a long life (Colour Plate 74). Furthermore, people often cut peonies in the background as a symbol of richness to mean "May you live long and prosper". Peony flowers also signify prosperity and nobility (Fig. 88).

Huafengsanzhu (Wishing You the Three Plenties)

The three plenties are plenty of money,

86. *Shuangquan*, double good luck.

87. A pillow decoration symbolizing good
fortune and longevity.

Liannianyouyu (May You Have More Than Enough Every Year.)

This proverb uses the pun on *lian* which can mean both lotus and continuous, and on *yu* which means a surplus, but also means fish (Fig. 89). It is often painted as a child hugging a big fish with a lotus flower in his hand. This image is found not only in papercuts, but also in folk woodblock prints (Fig. 90). The motif of a child and a lotus flower had its origins in the Buddhist scriptures as a reincarnation theme, and can be found in the Dunhuang wall paintings of the Sui-Tang period (581-907). During the Song Dynasty its uses were expanded to pottery and brocade, and it is a common ornamental theme in traditional art work.

Guadiemianmian (Continuous Prosperity)

This comes from a poem in the *Book of Songs*. The idea of continuity is expressed by *die* (tendrils of a melon). Papercut artisans have

89. "May riches fill your house"
—a window ornament.

88. A window ornament symbolizing longevity and prosperity.

plenty of years to your life and plenty of sons. The story for this saying comes from the second century B.C. from the works of the famous philosopher Zhuang Zi. It is said that there was a sagacious emperor, Tang Yao, who went to inspect the border region Hua, and when he got there the man enfeoffed (*feng*) there wished him "three plenties" (*sanzhu*). In papercuts, this story is often represented by a *fu* (in the form of the bergamot), a peach to symbolize longevity, and a pomegranate to symbolize many sons (Colour Plate 68). A pomegranate has hundreds of tiny seeds, *zi*, also the word for sons. Hence the saying "Open a pomegranate and see happiness."

added another *die* (butterfly) to the design (Fig. 91).

Shishiruyi (May Everything Proceed According to Your Wishes)

Using the pun of *shi* (meaning matter or affair, and also persimmon) these cuts intertwine a persimmon with a *ruyi* (Fig. 92).

Zhubaoping'an (Bamboo Announces That All Is Well)

According to ancient records, in Shanxi Province there was a temple with a clump of bamboo. Since bamboo usually grows in the south where the climate is suitable, to find bamboo in this northern temple was very unusual, and the monks went to see it every day. They reported its condition to the people of the area. Later people used this proverb to report their safety to their families when they were away from home or to express their wishes for a peaceful life. Chinese have traditionally loved bamboo not only because it has a graceful appearance, but also because it is homophonous with the word for wishing good luck, adding an extra layer of meaning to the proverb. Papercuts on this subject depict a single stalk of bamboo standing straight with brilliant green leaves, or depict a certain kind of fireworks made from bamboo and used to celebrate the New Year (Fig. 93).

Xishizaiqian (There Will Be Immediate Good Luck)

This good-luck picture shows a magpie (*xi-que*) lifting his head to sing, standing on a persimmon branch (*shi*, homophonous with the word for affair), and in between the persimmon and the magpie sits a patterned

90. "May you have more than enough every year"—a window ornament.

91. *Guadiemianmian*, a symbol meaning continuous prosperity.

48

92. This is a composite of three paper cuts which mean "May everything proceed according to your wishes," "May you enjoy prosperity and a long life," and "May you have many promising sons."

93. "All Is Well"—a pillow decoration.

piece of money (*qian*, homophonous with the word for the immediate future) (Colour Plate 72). Another good-luck papercut shows a magpie standing on a plum tree (Fig. 94).

Sijunzihua (The Four Gentlemen Flowers)

Among Chinese plants, the four "gentleman flowers" are the plum blossom, the orchid, bamboo and the chrysanthemum. A gentleman is a person who is both well educated and moral, and traditionally the qualities of these flowers have been used to symbolize those of a gentleman in Chinese poetry and painting. The plum blossom braves the frost and is the first to open in the spring; the orchid secludes itself deep in mountain valleys and does not care if no one can appreciate its fragrance; bamboo symbolizes moral fortitude and incorruptibility; and the chrysanthemum is called the recluse flower. Because these plants are also beautiful, they are often used in ornamentation, and in papercuts can be seen individually and together expressing these themes (Fig. 95).

Suihansanyou (The Three Friends of Winter)

It is said that "the three friends of winter are pine, bamboo and plum". These three plants are resistant to the cold and have become a metaphor for strength of moral purpose and character. They are often depicted together in papercuts (Fig. 96).

94. A pillow decoration meaning that "there will be immediate good luck."

95. "The Four Gentleman Flowers"
—window ornaments.

Luhetongchun (Spring Comes to the World.)

Luhe means the heaven, the earth and the four directions, or the world. In papercuts it is symbolized by deer (*lu*) and crane (*he*), two homophonous characters. Together, *luhetong-chun* signifies that life and prosperity return in spring (Fig. 97).

Traditional Fairy Tales and Characters

Over the course of Chinese history there have developed wonderful fairy stories and tales of heros and famous events. Some of these stories are reliable and some are simply passed down by word of mouth from generation to generation, slowly becoming part of the people's literature and material for popular plays and operas. Papercuts are another medium for telling these traditional stories and are meant to eulogize these characters' high moral qualities and sense of patriotism to set examples for people to follow. Of course these papercuts also reveal the tastes and creative

97. *Luhetongchun*—a pillow decoration.

96. "The Three Friends of Winter"—
a "happiness" ornament.

50

spirit of the people who make them. Some of the most famous stories are as follows:

Carp Jump over Dragon's Gate

The famous Ming Dynasty scholar of Chinese medicine Li Shizhen (1518-1593), in his famous work *Compendium of Materia Medica*, writes: "Carp is the king of fish. Its shape is attractive, and it has the ability to transform itself and fly over the rivers and lakes, which is why the fairy Qin Gao rides carp." The carp of the Yellow River are the most famous. Swimming upstream they get to the place called Dragon's Gate where both banks of the river are steep and dangerous. From there they continue up the river not by swimming but by leaping through the air. According to folk tradition, when carp pass through Dragon's Gate they become dragons. Therefore, people have used this story to mean someone who has been promoted or has become extremely famous and successful. This scene is depicted in papercuts quite frequently, usually by cutting a Chinese-style gate with waves crashing around it and fish leaping through the air (Colour Plate 70) (Fig. 98).

Chang E Flies to the Moon

This is one of the oldest fairy tales. Chang E was the wife of the famous fairy-tale warrior Hou Yi. Hou Yi received an immortality potion from the Heavenly Queen Mother. Knowing the way Hou Yi oppressed his people and fearing the consequences of his immortality, Chang E stole the potion and drank it herself, and then escaped to the moon. In history Chang E's name is not entirely heroic, but in the popular mind she represents the beauty of the moon. Often depicted with her in the moon palace are the jade hare and the cassia tree (Colour Plate 77).

98. "Carp Jumps over Dragon's Gate."

The Meeting on Magpie Bridge

Also called "The Cowherd and the Weaver Woman", this story is based around the two Chinese constellations of the same names. The weaver woman was the granddaughter of the emperor of the heavens, and had the ability to make beautiful fabrics. She married a mortal, cowherd from west of the Heavenly River (Milky Way), and when this was discovered, her grandfather called her back from earth and would only allow her to see her husband once a year (on the seventh day of the seventh lunar month). Magpies, who heard the lamenting of the unhappy couple, took pity on them and on that day they make a bridge across the Heavenly River for the two to meet on. Papercuts of this story often depict this scene (Fig. 99).

The Goddess Scatters Flowers

This story first appeared in the Buddhist scriptures, and tells of the goddess of heaven who wanted to test the morality of the Bodhisattvas and their disciples. She scattered

99. "The Meeting on Magpie Bridge."

flowers, and those disciples on whom flowers fell and stayed she knew had not yet reached perfection. In folk cuts of this story, people have changed the meaning somewhat, and it has come to signify happiness in general (Colour Plate 118). The Tang Dynasty poet Song Zhiwen (about 656-712) has said: "The goddess scatters flowers to decorate the grasses and trees in mountain forest", that is, to make nature even more beautiful through ornamentation.

Eight Immortals Cross the Sea

Traditional stories include tales of Eight Immortals, each with a different kind of magic weapon which he or she is the master of. Their story is known everywhere, but it was not until the Ming Dynasty that their names were set down. To go to the heavenly gathering held by the Heavenly Queen Mother, each carried his or her magic instrument and crossed the sea which separated heaven and earth. This scene has since become a proverb "the Eight Immortals cross the sea, each displaying his or her own prowess", and is used to describe a group of individuals with different talents. Most folk papercuts of this story cut each immortal individually (Colour Plates 78, 85, 86) (Fig. 100).

Ma Gu Wishes the Heavenly Queen Mother Long Life

Ma Gu is a fairy in traditional tales, so youthful and beautiful that she could transform rice kernels into pearls simply by throwing them into the air. On one occasion she went out to pick magic medicinal herbs which she made into a kind of wine with ganoderma, and offered to the Heavenly Queen Mother to wish her long life on her birthday. This scene is often depicted in papercuts (Fig. 101).

The Two Immortals of Harmony

These two immortals are often depicted with dishevelled hair, arms linked, dancing together, one holding a lotus (*he*) and the other holding a round box (*he*), puns on the words harmony (*he*) and unity (*he*), and used to symbolize love between husband and wife. In papercuts, this story is sometimes represented by a lotus and a round box alone, sometimes with a bat added to signify good fortune (Colour Plate 75).

Mice Marry Off Their Daughter

This is a folk story which personifies a group of mice and describes their marriages in vivid detail. One famous papercut of this story is four metres in width, and depicts the wedding ceremony, complete with drums and horns, the sedan chair which carries the bride, and a parade of one hundred mice. The bridegroom is strutting about puffed up with pride, and the whole scene is meant to be humorous (Colour Plate 76).

Characters from *Journey to the West*

The Ming Dynasty author Wu Cheng'en (1500-1582) describes the story of Monk Xuanzang, Sun Wukong (Monkey), Pig, and Friar Sand going to fetch Buddhist scriptures from the western heavens. Sun Wukong is the monkey king, capable of changing himself into many forms and of subduing evil spirits. He fears nothing and dares to fight with every opponent they meet, for his temperament is both rebellious and stubborn. Pig is lazy, stupid, selfish and narrow-minded, but straightforward, and good natured, and though the readers laugh at him, they also grow to love him. Most papercuts only depict these two characters, although all four of them are sometimes cut together (Colour Plates 79, 80).

100. Lü Dongbin, one of the Eight Immortals.

101. "Ma Gu Wishes the Heavenly Queen Mother Long Life."

Characters from *Outlaws of the Marsh*

Wu Song is one of the main characters in the Chinese classic *Outlaws of the Marsh*. A courageous hero, he dares fight all of the evil forces he comes upon, and at one point proves his valour by fighting the tiger of Jingyang Ridge. This story is deeply loved by the people and is often found in papercuts (Colour Plate 81).

Characters from *A Dream of Red Mansions*

Lin Daiyu is the heroine of the Qing Dynasty classic *A Dream of Red Mansions* by Cao Xueqin (?-1763), a wise but overly sensitive young girl from Suzhou. With her disdain for all things connected with money and power, she is left with a kind of lonely aloofness, revealed in the strange mixture of self-righteous distancing and complicated anxiety she feels for the world around her. There is one passage in the book which describes her sighing over the fate of the fallen flowers and burying them in a proper grave (Colour Plate 82).

Characters from *The Story of the Western Chamber*

The Story of the Western Chamber is a famous play written in the Yuan Dynasty by Wang Shifu. It tells the story of a student, Zhang Gong, who meets Ying Ying, the daughter of the deceased prime minister in a temple and falls in love with her. With the help of the clever servant girl, Hong Niang, the two are united. "The Whipping of Hong Niang" tells one of the incidents before the happy resolution of the story, when poor, kind Hong Niang is whipped and scolded by the stubborn and feudal mother of Ying Ying. Other events

from this play are also used as material for papercuts (Colour Plate 83).

Characters from *The Story of the White Snake*

The Story of the White Snake is a traditional opera whose plot comes from folk tales. It tells the story of the White Snake (or the White Maiden) who comes down from the mountain one day bored with her life above the earth and sets off with the Green Snake (Little Green) for Hangzhou. The White Maiden get married to Xu Xian there, but the evil monk Fahai takes them for evil spirits and tries to harm them. The story of water flooding the Gold Mountain Temple tells of the White Maiden's struggle with Fahai during which time the water surrounding the Gold Mountain Temple begins churning and the fish begin leaping, increasing the tension of the atmosphere. Papercuts of this opera also depict other scenes than the "battle on the water" (Colour Plate 84).

Liang and Zhu Change into Butterflies

The traditional opera called *Liang Shanbo and Zhu Yingtai* gets its material from popular folk tales. It tells of Zhu Yingtai, a woman who dressed up as a man, and Liang Shanbo, a man, who study together for three years and become the fastest of friends, Liang Shanbo never discovering that Zhu Yingtai is a woman. Just as they are about to finish their schooling and part ways, Zhu pretends she wants to introduce Liang to her younger sister, but Liang's father has already selected someone else for Liang and will not allow them to marry. The two young people are sacrificed to the oppressive system of feudal relations and die tragically. After their death, they turn into butterflies and fly away together (Fig. 102).

102. "Liang Shanbo and Zhu Yingtai."

Woman Warriors of the Yang Family

At the end of the Northern Song Dynasty there lived a family named Yang. The family produced several generations of famous generals, fighting to oppose the incursions by the Liao (a northern minority nationality). Tradition has it that these "Yang family generals" included women warriors, who have become well-loved and famous in the stories *The Western Expedition of Twelve Widows* and *Mu Guiying Takes Over the Command* (Fig. 103).

Zhaojun Journeys to the North

Wang Zhaojun was a concubine of Emperor Yuandi (76-33 B.C.) of the Western Han. In order to make peace with the warring Xiongnu tribe, a minority nationality from the north, she left her native land and journeyed to the north to marry the leader of the Xiongnu. This story has been turned into poems and operas, and the papercut of this usually depicts Zhaojun on her journey north (Colour Plate 87).

Su Wu Sent to Raise Sheep

Su Wu (?-60 B.C.) from Duling (in today's Shaanxi Province) during the Western Han period was sent on a mission to negotiate with the Xiongnu, and while he was there he was detained by them. The ruling class of the Xiongnu tried to force him to surrender, but his loyalty to the Han court never wavered. Finally the Xiongnu sent him to the "northern sea", that is today's Lake Baikal in Siberia, to be a shepherd for nineteen years. In the end, when the Xiongnu made peace with the Han, Su Wu was released. His story has been passed down these thousands of years, and is depicted in papercuts with him carrying a whip, standing in the fields surrounded by his sheep (Colour Plate 88).

Xizhi and His Geese

Wang Xizhi (321-379) was a famous calligrapher from the Eastern Jin Dynasty, whose characters were both fluid and vigorous. As the story goes, he loved geese, for he felt he could learn how to use his brush from

103. A woman warrior of the Yang family.

watching the way geese moved through water. People who wanted him to do writing for them began to raise flocks of geese to give to Wang Xizhi to watch, until this became an official form of trade "Geese for handwriting" (Fig. 104).

The Two Qiao Sisters Reading

During the Three Kingdoms period (220-280), Lord Qiao had two daughters, who were dazzling beauties. The elder was married to the famous general Sun Ce, while the younger was married to another famous general Zhou Yu, and the two together were called the two Qiaos. There are many popular stories about these two sisters (Fig. 105).

Tromping Through the Snow Looking for Plum Blossoms

The poet Lin Bu (967-1028) of the Northern Song lived in an isolated mountain area near West Lake, and loved plums and cranes, both symbols of reclusive purity. He never served as an official, nor did he ever take a wife, which is why people called him "the man with plum blossoms for a wife, and cranes for sons". His poems are subdued, and reflect the scenery of his lonely surroundings. During the bitter cold

105. "The Two Qiao Sisters Reading."

106. "Tromping Through the Snow Looking for Plum Blossoms"—a window ornament.

104. "Xizhi and His Geese."

56

and snow of winter, he insisted on "tromping through the snow to look for plum blossoms" riding on the back of his little donkey, and it is this scene that is most commonly depicted in papercuts (Fig. 106).

As can be seen from the above examples, the folklore involved in papercuts has thousands of years of history. But, papercuts are not only used to relate these traditional stories. More importantly, one finds papercuts beautifying those occasions most important to people's lives: marriage, the birth of children, the change of seasons and festivals all have expression in papercuts, either as ornaments or as gifts. For example, there is the tradition of holding dragon-boat race and ridding the house of vermins such as scorpions, centipedes and poisonous snakes on the fifth day of the fifth lunar month when the weather gets warm. These activities are also expressed in papercuts (Colour Plates 89, 90). Papercut bottle gourds, traditional containers of medicine, are made to remain people to pay attention to hygiene. A walk through a country town on Spring Festival, Dragon Boat Festival, Mid-Autumn Festival or during a New Year's fair or temple bazzar is the ideal way to see the spirit of the people take form in these exuberant works of art.

4. The Techniques of Papercutting

Tools and Materials (Fig. 107)

Needless to say, though the material used is the same, cutting paper with scissors and cutting with a knife use different tools and hence different techniques. Furthermore, cutting with a knife also requires a pan with wax in it, a grindstone and a bag of powder.

Scissors: Ordinary scissors from the department store usually both a medium-sized and a small pair are all one needs to cut paper using this technique. The medium-sized scissors are used for the outlines and the larger lines, and the smaller scissors for the delicate lines and details. The scissors should be sharp and should have pointed cutting blades. Using scissors, though it does not require many tools, is difficult to do well.

Knife: The kind of knife usually used is a sharp-pointed slanted knife, usually in both large and small sizes. Professional artisans use specially made knives, with an especially tough point. If you make one yourself, you can use a used metal saw blade or an alarm clock spring and grind it down to a slanted edge for one of the knives, and a less slanted edge for the other. It should be five to seven millimetres in width, about ten centimetres in length and the cutting edge should be double-bevelled. After it has been ground down, it should be mounted on a bamboo handle with string.

Wax pan: Also known as an oil pan, it is put underneath the paper when cutting with a knife to make the cut run more smoothly. It is made using powder and beef oil or vaseline, or from wax and rubber cement. To make, mix the ingredients together in a pan and heat until they melt. The pan can be made from thin pieces of wood hammered together into a box about 25 centimetres long, 20 centimetres wide and 3 centimetres deep. The melted ingredients are then pressed into the pan and levelled. To tell if the wax is hard enough, press your finger on it and make sure it leaves no impression.

If you do not have a wax pan you may use a thick piece of cardboard or a piece of soft wood, but these materials cannot be re-used as many times.

Grindstone: Used to sharpen knives. It is best to have two stones, one coarse and the other fine. A brick can also be used, and oilstone is the best. When grinding a knife one must make sure to grind both side of the cutting edge equally, to insure sharpness.

Powder bag: Use a square piece of finely cloth, and put water chestnut, sweet potato or talcum powder into it. Tie it with a thread, and spread a thin layer on the wax pan before beginning to cut to prevent the paper sticking to the wax.

Paper: In general, the kinds of paper can be divided into three categories: The first is ordinary solid-colour paper, preferably *maobian*, a kind of calligraphy paper made from young bamboo which has been treated with lime and then pounded into pulp and drained with a bamboo screen. The original paper is a

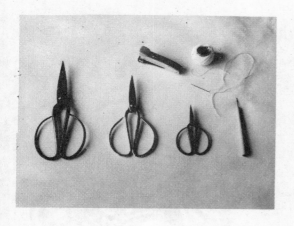

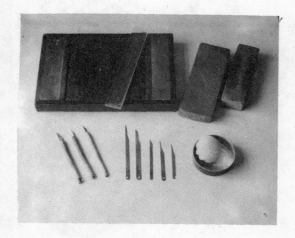

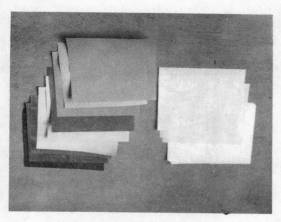

107. Tools and materials used in papercutting.

light yellow colour, patterned with the impressions of the bamboo screen. It can be dyed any colour, and as it is thick and not shiny it is perfect for papercuts. Aside from *maobian* paper, newsprint with colour brushed on it can also be used; there is also a kind of shiny paper, though the shine is not even the effect is not good. The second kind of paper, *Xuan* or *lianshi*, famous traditional papers are coloured or otherwise worked after the cut. The third possibility is to cut tin or aluminium foil to make gold and silver leaf, which can then be used to decorate coloured papercuts.

Besides the few tools and materials mentioned above, there are certain tools used for particular procedures. In cutting paper with a knife sometimes a triangle knife or a circle knife is useful for cutting those shapes. For small holes a sewing needle is useful or a hypodermic needle ground down to size. The other materials like needle and thread or paints are easily found.

The Basic Skills

Techniques for Chinese papercutting are many and various, but we can divide them into the following categories.

1. *Folding*: Folding the paper to produce repeated patterns when cutting is the most basic technique of the art and is only used for solid coloured paper. Of course, depending on how many times the paper is folded, a great variety of effects can be produced by this one method (Fig. 108) from simple symmetry of a single fold, to the complicated repetitions produced by many folds (Fig. 109). The oldest papercuts discovered to date all use this method.

2. *Negative and positive lines*: The basic effect of papercutting is produced through single or mixed use of negative and positive lines. Negative lines mean that the outline of the object to be cut is made by a lack of paper, by

108. Simple symmetry is achieved by a single fold.

109. Repetitions produced by four folds.

the cut away spaces (Fig. 110). Positive lines, then, outline the object to be depicted with lines of paper leaving the inside and less important places to be cut away (Fig. 110 upper), as with the embroidery stencils of the famous papercut artisan Zhang Yongshou. When both of these cutting methods are used together (Fig. 110 lower), cutting or not cutting according to the needs of the design and the contents of the picture, the effect is

110. A pigeon depicted in positive lines (*upper*), negative lines (*middle*) and combined positive and negative lines (*lower*).

more complicated and is called "black and white outlining each other".

3. *Perforation*: A third method is to cut out the basic outline with a knife or scissors and then use a needle to perforate the finer designs, giving people a feeling of seeing the refined in the coarse. This method is commonly used among the Miao minority of Guizhou Province (Fig. 111).

4. *Solid colours, many colours and patchwork*: Generally speaking, all cuts made to be hung or stuck up directly are cut from bright coloured paper — red, green, yellow or blue — while those made to be stencils are cut from plain white paper. Positive, negative or combined positive and negative lines can be used. Patchwork can also be used, which means after various parts of the whole are cut, they are pieced together to form the design, as with a flower where the flower itself is cut out in red and pieced to the leaves which have been cut out in green (Colour plates 91-92). This method of patchwork papercuts has not been popular for long, but can be seen in Shandong Province's Jiaoxian County and in the Pujiang region of Zhejiang. The rules for piecing are not at all set; as long as a complete cut is left on which to attach the various colours, any sort of arrangement of colours is acceptable, and the same cut can be made with different arrangements of colours, to avoid repetition. This kind of cut can be seen in the incense burner decorations of Nanjing (Colour plates 93-94) and in the door hangings of Shandong folk cuts (Colour plates 95, 97).

5. *Background colours*: Simply put, different

111. The finer designs of a cuff ornament are perforated with a needle.

61

coloured pieces of paper are placed as background for a completed cut. However, there are variants of this method worth noting: the first is to place a bright colour under the cut so that the contrast is even more stunning than the individual colours. The second is to place different background colours under different parts of the cut according to the needs of the design and the contents; the third is to place background colours not according to the design of the cut, but according to any pattern one likes, so that the background competes with the paper cut for the eye's attention. The second method is most commonly seen in folk cuts.

No matter which background method is used, the papercut to be mounted must be cut in a single colour, but the papercut colour should be neither too light nor too bright. Usually black or gold foil are used. Furthermore, positive lines should be used to show off the background colours. The Foshan region in Guangdong Province has a kind of papercut which uses gold foil for the main pattern and puts red, rose, apricot, bright green or deep blue behind as a background. In the past, Wuxi in Jiangsu Province had a kind of papercut which used black paper for the pattern and shiny coloured paper as a background (Colour plates 98, 100).

6. *Hand colouring*: This method involves colouring the completed papercut in various ways using the same pigments used for dyeing material — green, red, yellow, purple or blue — but putting the pigments in alcohol first to increase their permeability. The papercuts using this method are all cut with a knife, and are usually window ornaments. These cuts must be principally made from negative lines, leaving large areas of paper to be dyed. The paper used can be *xuan* or *lianshi* paper, since these papers are thin and will absorb water easily, allowing a single dot of colour to spread out without leaving a mark. The pigments used for this colouring process should be extremely bright. The end results resemble folk woodblock prints, and the most famous examples are found in Yuxian, Hebei Province (Colour plates 101-104, 106, 109-112, 116).

7. *Hand-painted details*: This method involves both papercutting and painting. With the papercut as a basis, one can use a brush to outline the details, for example, of facial features of human characters, the stamen of flowers or the veins of leaves, or to outline the entire design and then use scissors to cut out the spaces. By still a third technique, one cuts the general outline out of silver or gold foil and then paints onto the paper put behind as background. The former kind of cut is elegant and peaceful looking, and is found in the Jiaodong area of Shandong as window ornaments (Colour plate 114). The latter is more flashy and can be found in the Foshan area of Guangdong (Colour plate 115). These two methods of papercutting have used the techniques of painting, while retaining the special characteristics of papercuts.

8. *Woodblock-printed details*: Papercuts which use this method come out looking quite a bit like New Year pictures. These cuts are often of human figures, making them rather more difficult, especially when it comes to cutting the facial features. If positive lines are used they must all be connected, which, if not done properly, can look unclear and chaotic; if negative lines are used, there is often too much paper left and the effect is dark and smeared. Probably for these reasons, people have used woodblocks to stamp out these details. Examples of this technique can be found in the incense burner decorations from Nanjing in Jiangsu, and in Wuxi's gift ornaments (Colour plate 116). The region of Huangxian and Zhaoyuan in Shandong Province also has a kind of window ornament that is made entirely by woodblock printing, printing first and cutting out after. This kind of window decoration usually tell stories of historical

characters. Some of them are hung up after printing and cutting, while others are further coloured before put up to ornament the house.

The Basic Steps

The tools and materials involved in papercutting are simple, and consequently the steps in papercutting cannot be too complicated. Nevertheless, there is a certain order to the procedure, and steps cannot be overlooked or taken out of turn. In general these steps can be described as choosing a model, securing the paper; cutting and finally mounting the paper.

Choosing a model: When making a papercut, no matter whether it is a duplication or an original creation you must have an overall plan. Particularly for original cuts, you must have a detailed design in mind if you want satisfactory results.

In folk paper cutting, duplication and original creation are not necessarily two distinct processes, and rarely is a cut completely duplicated or completely original. Peasant women often exchange stencils, but then add their own touches changing the effect slightly. The popularization and progress of Chinese papercuts depend on this process of minute but significant change and personalization.

In folk papercutting, peasants use one of two methods for copying the stencil onto the paper to be cut: the first is smoking, the second is rubbing. Smoking involves wetting the model and then sticking it to a piece of paper and putting the whole paper over an oil lamp to smoke. When the original model is removed the white lines it delineates are clear and the paper can be cut directly (Fig. 112). Rubbing involves pressing the paper tightly against the model and then using a special kind of black wax to rub the pattern. The surface upon which you rub should be level to make a clear black

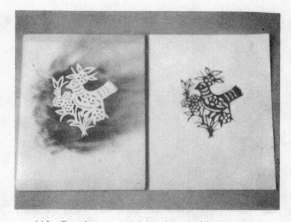

112. Copying a model by the smoking method.

outline. The special kind of black wax is made from paraffin wax and pine soot heated together, an ancient process which papercutters still use today (Fig. 113).

For making the original design, it does not matters which tools you use — calligraphy brushes or pencils will do. Whether or not the design will work for a papercut depends on the way the lines connect and the arrangement of white and black. Both must be fitting and natural. Usually both papercuts of animals and papercuts of people use profile views to make the most of papercuts' emphasis on outline and

113. Copying a model by rubbing.

"shadow drawing", and the methods of approximation and exaggeration must be used skilfully, with appropriate ornament added after the basic structure of the cut has been made clear. Flowers and plants can be cut straight on, but the process of two-dimensionalization makes depiction complicated. As far as the thickness of the lines is concerned, the contrast between straight and curved lines and the empty and the solid must be carefully considered in the original stencil to make full use of the special properties of papercuts (Fig. 114).

114. Sketches of two original designs.

In preparing the model, it is necessary that the outlines and structural lines be clear and certain, never timid or indistinct, for the first cut determines the success or failure of the whole work, and there is no way to repair a cut gone wrong. Therefore, it is best not to draw a single fine line to delineate the outline of the papercut. Instead secure the paper and plan out precisely what thickness and direction the lines will take. This is particularly important for beginners who have not much experience.

Folk artisans who cut with scissors almost never follow a model, but instead cut from scratch, a skill which requires years of experience to perfect. Because individual artisans use a limited number of subjects and designs, they have cut similar cuts thousands and thousands of times, and are by no means picking their ideas out of thin air, nor can they simply cut anything they like.

Securing the paper: Securing the model and the paper to be cut is one of the necessary steps in papercutting. Excluding the plain white or black paper used in painting the paper or making papercuts with backgrounds, most papercuts can be made with any or many colours of paper according to the contents of the design to be cut. When using scissors, one cut can be done on four or five pieces of paper simultaneously. A knife can accommodate about ten layers of paper or so. When folk artisans make door hangings they can cut as many as fifty hangings at a time. Usually the number of papers to be cut at one go depends both on the intricacy of the cut and on the skill of the artist.

When folk artisans secure their paper they usually use the method of pinching: this involves a long triangular piece of paper rolled into a peg which is threaded through a hole pierced in the paper and tightened. Thread and needle or staples can also be used to fasten the paper together (Fig. 115). Following the design, secure each corner and areas to be cut to keep the paper as flat as possible. Of course,

115. Securing the paper.

one should be careful not to pierce a hole in the design. After the paper and stencil are secured, the process of cutting can begin.

If the paper is to be folded and cut, not only must the number and position of the folds be calculated into the design, but the folds must be even or else the resulting cut will look lopsided.

Cutting: Cutting with scissors is the more difficult of the two ways to cut paper. Without enough practice the lines come out crooked and rough. Cutting with a knife is easier, and a little practice can produce satisfactory results.

To use scissors, it is helpful to remember one of the phrases of the trade: "follow the sissors". This means that one should cut from outside to inside then to outside again, so that the entire cut is made without lifting the scissors (Fig. 116). One should try to avoid having to dig the scissors into the paper to start a space, and in cases where hollowing is absolutely necessary, try to use the method of following the scissors to cut over the hollowed place. This method is extremely intricate, and rarely does anyone but a folk artisan truly master it. Most cuts by peasant women are of single pieces of paper and involve lifting the scissors and digging out a new hole. Though this method takes a little longer, it puts to full use the characteristics of the scissors, as can be seen in the saw tooth border effect of so many of the most successful

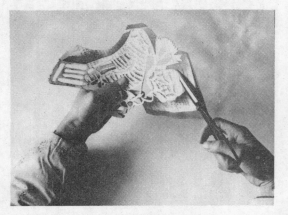

116. Cutting from outside to inside.

papercut, use glue to paste each corner and select points on the interior of the cut. Pay particular attention to unconnected lines which curl up if they are not individually fastened. A piece of cardboard can be cut into the shape of a triangle and used to spread the glue by inserting the cardboard under the places to be glued without lifting the paper itself (Fig. 119).

2. If the area to be glued is fairly large and the lines are fairly thick the cut can be turned over and glue applied directly, then a piece of

papercuts (Fig. 117).

Using a knife the order of the steps is also very important and cannot be done at random. Cutting should procede from inside to outside and from fine to thick lines, ending with the cutting of the outline. There are two difficult points which must be paid great attention to in the use of the knife: the first is opening and finishing a cut, which requires that the knife be straight — the back straight when beginning a cut and the point straight when finishing a cut. Furthermore, the beginnings and endings of all lines must occur at the turning points of the cut. The second point to remember is that the movement of the knife must be absolutely straight and cannot slant to either side. There are two ways to move the knife as well, one cutting with the knife blade pointing downwards, the other pushing with the knife blade pointing upwards, but these two methods are interchangeable. The only thing one should not do is "slide" the knife for this method does not make a clean cut and can easily go off course, producing lines where they are not wanted (Fig. 118).

Mounting: Once the papercut is finished it must be pasted on a piece of white paper using one of various methods.

1. After fastening the position of the

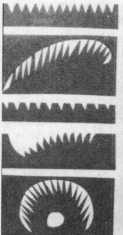

117. Types of cuts.

118. Cutting with a knife.

119. Mounting a papercut.

portion, but this methods is not suitable for cuts which are too large or too complicated.

4. Mounting. This method of pasting is rather complicated, and involves first spreading the background paper on a board and wetting it, then covering it with a thin layer of paste, then placing the paper cuts on it. Taking a second piece of dry paper, place it on top of the entire work and brush the surface flat with a palm-fibre brush, then quickly remove the second piece of paper which has absorbed most of the excess paste. Finally attach the four corners of the background paper to a board and dry and level it. This mounting process makes the papercut more secure, but it takes a lot of time and is not easy to master.

5. If there are many pieces of background paper to be pieced together they must be pasted securely first before the papercut can be pasted on top of them.

white paper can be placed on top and press the papercut flat.

3. Some people prefer papercuts loosely pasted, by, for example, only pasting the top

《中国民间剪纸艺术》

张道一　著

*

外文出版社出版

(中国北京百万庄路 24 号)

外文印刷厂印刷

中国国际图书贸易总公司

(中国国际书店)发行

北京 399 信箱

1989 年(16 开)第一版

(英)

ISBN 7-119-00791-2／G・17 (外)

01740

7-E-1828P